Women of the Frontier

OTHER BOOKS IN THE
WOMEN OF ACTION SERIES

Double Victory: How African American Women Broke Race and Gender Barriers to Help Win World War II

Women Heroes of World War II: 26 Stories of Espionage, Sabotage, Resistance, and Rescue

WOMEN *of the* FRONTIER

16 Tales of Trailblazing Homesteaders, Entrepreneurs, and Rabble-Rousers

Brandon Marie Miller

First edition
Published by Chicago Review Press, Incorporated
814 North Franklin Street
Chicago, Illinois 60610

ISBN 978-1-883052-97-3

Parts of this work were originally published as *Buffalo Gals: Women of the Old West* (Minneapolis, MN: Lerner Publishing, 1995). They have been substantially revised, updated, and expanded.

Interior design: Sarah Olson
Map design: Chris Erichsen

Library of Congress Cataloging-in-Publication Data
Miller, Brandon Marie.
Women of the frontier : 16 tales of trailblazing homesteaders, entrepreneurs, and rabble-rousers / Brandon Marie Miller. — 1st ed.
p. cm.
Includes bibliographical references and index.
ISBN 978-1-883052-97-3 (hardcover)
1. Women pioneers—West (U.S.)—History—Biography—Juvenile literature.
2. West (U.S.)—History—Biography—Juvenile literature. I. Title.

CT3262.W37M55 2013
978'.033082—dc23

2012035756

Printed in the United States of America
5 4 3 2 1

For Paul, with love

(Boy Justin and Tom, too. Now I've gotten to everyone!)

CONTENTS

AUTHOR'S NOTE

As I researched this book, I often wondered how I'd react to the conditions these frontier women dealt with. At best, I'm afraid I would have complained a lot; at worst, I would have given up, running back to Ohio if so much as a snake fell through the roof of my sod house.

But the women on these pages persevered. Margret Reed and Rachel Plummer's stories haunted me. The determination of Luzena Wilson and Dr. Bethenia Owens-Adair humbled me. The eloquence of Susette La Flesche's fight for Native American rights moved me. And Carry Nation, whom I prejudged as a prudish old Puritan, made me laugh.

Most of the women here were not famous; they led ordinary lives as daughters, sisters, wives, and mothers. Thousands more shared these same stories but left no written record and today are nameless and forgotten. I pay tribute to every one of them.

1 MANY A WEARY MILE

"I have not told you half we suffered. I am not adequate to the task."[1]

—Elizabeth Smith Geer, the trail's end, 1847

Not long after sunrise on a May day in 1841, a dozen jam-packed covered wagons rumbled out of a small town along the Missouri River. Ox teams pulled the wagons steadily westward toward the Pacific coast, carting the baggage of 69 men, women, and children. Dawn rose behind their backs, but that night the sun would set ahead of them, a sign of hope beyond the horizon. They were the first trickle in a flood of pioneers, lured by the promise of better lives in the American West.

Americans had always looked west for escape and refuge. The lure of Western lands symbolized health, wealth, and freedom.

In 1837, the United States plunged into an economic depression as banks closed their doors and thousands of unemployed workers crowded Eastern cities. Farm prices plummeted, and many people lost their land. Adding to the sense of despair were the yellow fever, malaria, typhoid, and tuberculosis that ravaged the country year after year.

Eastern audiences devoured the published journals of fur trappers and explorers, in awe over their glorified western adventures. Letters from Oregon missionaries excited trouble-weary Americans. To many readers, the missionaries' tales of religious zeal paled next to their descriptions of rich farmland and forests, crystal waters abundant with fish, and hordes of animals awaiting fur trappers. News of miraculous cures in the West's pristine air offered great hope. Societies sprang up to encourage settlement of the Oregon country and California, too, praised as an earthly paradise of sunshine and lush fruit. One woman summed up the dreams of many: "We had nothing to lose, and we might gain a fortune."[2]

The temptation of cheap land in paradise proved hard to resist. During the spring of 1842, another 200 people traveled west. A year later, 1,000 optimistic settlers braved the journey. After the 1848 discovery of gold in California, the numbers exploded to 30,000 in 1849 and 55,000 in 1850. The Wilson family abandoned their Missouri farm in 1849 for the California gold fields: "So we came," wrote wife Luzena, "young, strong, healthy, hopeful, but penniless, into the new world."[3] Thousands of European immigrants, mainly from Germany, the British Isles, and Scandinavia, also joined the hopefuls heading west.

Most pioneers, especially those heading to the goldfields of California, were single men. But families and a handful of single women undertook the western journey, too. Of the 50,000 people journeying west in 1852, about 7,000 were women.

John Sutter's mill, Sacramento, California. The discovery of gold here led to a gold rush of emigrants. *From* Story of the Great Republic *by Helene Guerber*

To meet the emigrants' needs, publishers churned out manuals like *The National Wagon Road Guide* and *The Emigrants' Guide to Oregon and California*. Unfortunately, too many guidebooks proved dangerously unreliable. One manual even assured readers that notions of toil, hardship, and danger on the trail grew from their "own fruitful imagination."[4] And though women, too, studied the manuals, the books offered hardly a word of advice for female pioneers. Women were left to discover on their own how to cook, clean, dress, camp, and care for children on the long adventure.

Usually, the man of the household decided to pull up stakes and move his family west. While women shared the hope for a better life, many found it painful to leave their homes and sever ties, perhaps forever, with family, friends, and communities. Pushing beyond the established boundaries of the United States, early pioneers were emigrants to a foreign, mostly uncharted, land. California and the Southwest belonged to Mexico. The United States and Great Britain both claimed the Oregon Country, an area so large it included six future states. These faraway lands were already the home of Native Americans and people of Spanish decent. White Americans often viewed both groups with a mixture of fear and scorn.

A woman's journey west carried an added burden, coming at a time of life when she might be pregnant or caring for young children. The prospect of abandoning society to face months of heat, dust, storms, and "savage" Indians filled many women with dread and misgivings. "I have been reading the various guides of the route to California," wrote Lodisa Frizzell. "They have not improved my ideas of the *pleasure* of the trip."[5] Luzena Wilson recalled her feelings: "My husband grew enthusiastic and wanted to start immediately, but I would not be left behind. I thought where he could go I could, and where I went I could take my two little toddling babies. . . . I little realized then the task I had undertaken."[6]

One bride, days away from departing for a "jumping off" spot in Missouri, sang these hymn lyrics at her ceremony: "Can I bid you farewell? / Can I leave you, Far in heathen lands to dwell?" Another young woman, filled with youthful enthusiasm, viewed the trip as an adventure with "castles of shining gold"[7] waiting at the end. Helen Carpenter, a bride of four months, recorded, "Ho—for California—at last we are on the way and with good luck may someday reach the 'promised land.'"[8]

Faced with the decision to head west, people tackled the journey in several ways. Some booked passage on a ship and sailed around South America to California. Others traveled to

Panama, cut across the isthmus, and then sailed up the Pacific coast. By the late 1860s, railroad lines stretched across the continent and provided the quickest, if most expensive, way to travel.

Without much baggage but themselves, many single women opted for dusty, bumpy stagecoaches. Stops along the way featured crowded rooms and meals of questionable quality. Between 1856 and 1860, nearly 3,000 Mormon emigrants *walked* the brutal journey, pulling two-wheeled handcarts laden with goods, all the way from Iowa to Utah.

By far the most popular means of family transportation was the oxen-drawn covered wagon, built of seasoned hardwood and waterproofed with caulk and tar. An application of oil rainproofed the wagon's thick canvas covering. Spare parts—axles, wheels, spokes, and wagon tongues—hung beneath the wagon bed. Other necessities, like water barrels, grease buckets, and

A Mormon handcart company traveling to Utah. *US History Images*

rope, were lashed to the wagon sides. Finished, the covered wagon measured about 4 feet wide and 10 to 12 feet long, large enough to haul roughly 2,500 pounds of supplies and requiring 8 to 10 oxen to pull.

The journey required months of preparations before the wagon sat stuffed with tools, cookware, clothes, bedding, sewing supplies, guns and ammunition, medicines, a few luxuries, and food. Guidebooks recommended each emigrant carry 200 pounds of flour, 150 pounds of bacon, 10 pounds of coffee, 10 pounds of sugar, and 10 pounds of salt as well as staples like dried beans and fruit, rice, tea, pickles, baking soda, cornmeal, and vinegar.

Buying wagons and ox teams and then outfitting the whole project cost between $600 and $1,000. Travelers also needed ready cash to buy supplies along the way, pay ferry costs across rivers, and help establish their new homes. Seeking the promised lands of the West proved too costly for the nation's poor.

Across the Wide Missouri

Families traveled from their homes in Eastern states to perch on the edge of civilization in Missouri River towns, near the head of the Oregon Trail. More than 350,000 pioneers eventually traveled this main artery west between 1843 and the late 1860s. In places like Independence and Saint Joseph, Missouri, and Council Bluffs, Iowa, passing emigrants snatched up last-minute supplies, repaired wagons, and sought advice. Families and solo travelers banded together into larger groups for protection on the trail.

The first leg of the Oregon Trail followed the meandering Platte River toward the Rocky Mountains. Oxen plodded over the plains, slowing climbing to South Pass in Wyoming

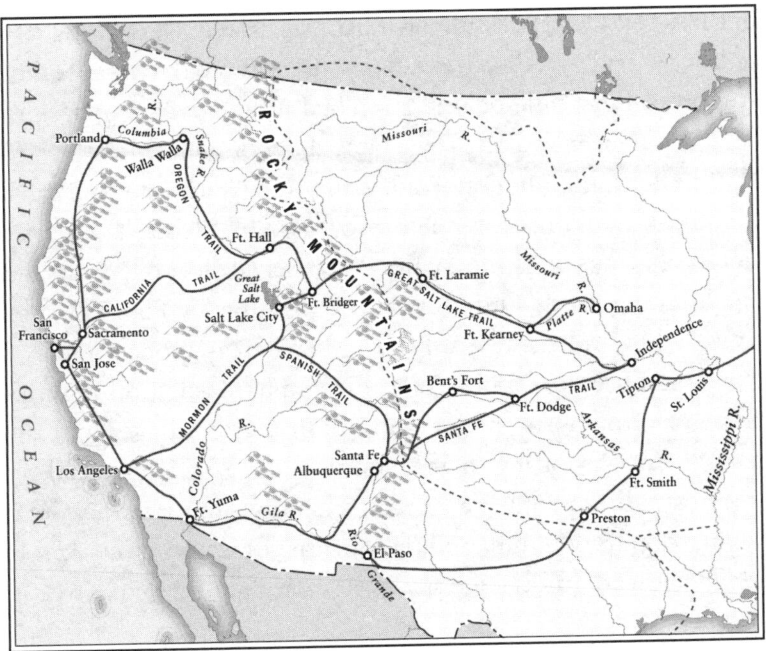

Map of the overland trails. *US History Images*

Territory and the Continental Divide—the boundary between eastward and westward flowing waters. Beyond the Rockies, the trail forked into two routes, one continuing northward along the Snake River in Oregon Country (Idaho, today), the other offshoot following the Humboldt River heading toward California. Emigrants to Southern California followed the Santa Fe Trail from Missouri to a split near Santa Fe in New Mexico Territory. The Old Spanish Trail carried on to Los Angeles and the Gila River Trail to San Diego.

On any route, travel proved slow and monotonous as the wagon trains covered only 10 to 20 miles each day. One woman reported that most people in her party had lost track of the days of the week. "Still pressing onward," she noted. "It is a long and tedious journey."[9] Ahead, clouds of dust marked the trail of other wagon trains, while behind stretched more advancing parties, weaving their way along the routes abandoning civilization.

All along the Oregon Trail, emigrants watched eagerly for landmarks announcing their progress. In Nebraska, diaries noted sightings of Chimney Rock soaring 500 feet overhead and the looming Scotts Bluff. Just into Wyoming lay Fort Laramie, followed by Independence Rock, where many pioneers carved their names, and Devil's Gate. Emigrants dashed off descriptions of pronghorn antelope and prairie dog villages and the excitement of spotting their first herd of great shaggy buffalo.

Most white people had never seen anything like the Great Plains: oceans of tough, undulating grass as far as one could see, a huge bowl of milky-blue sky overhead, and often not a tree in

Emigrant wagon train on the road to California, 1850. *Library of Congress*

sight. This hardly looked like a paradise to the early emigrants. The land seemed a fit home only for Indians. Later pioneers, hungry for free land, willingly settled the arid plains stretching from North Dakota down to Texas and west to parts of Wyoming, Colorado, and Montana.

Guidebooks warned travelers that the journey was "one in which time is everything." Leaving in spring, when there was grass enough to feed the livestock, settlers raced against the onset of winter, facing more than 2,000 miles to the Pacific coast. If they delayed too long, deadly snows would trap them in the mountains that stretched like a wall before Oregon and California.

While the guidebooks promised a three- or four-month journey, six months or even eight months of grueling travel proved nearer to the truth. Camping, cooking, laundry, exhaustion, and illness marked the journey. Days began before sunrise with cooking and eating breakfast, packing up tents and bedding, and yoking animals to wagons. After a noon break, travel continued to the next camp; the best sites provided clean water, grass, and wood. Emigrants turned the animals loose inside a circle of wagons, milked cows, pitched the tents, cooked supper, and cleaned up. After enjoying visits with fellow travelers and sharing a bit of music around the campfire, they tumbled into bed, utterly spent.

Each day followed in a dreary sameness. Throughout the trip, women struggled to keep a semblance of home and family life, but nothing about life on the trail proved ordinary.

"Done Brave"

Cooking, the most basic daily chore, was now done stooping over an open campfire. It was a far cry from cooking back home on a wood-stoked stove with familiar utensils and a full box of kindling close at hand. "Although there is not much to cook," lamented Helen Carpenter, "the difficulty and inconvenience in doing it, amounts to a great deal."[10]

The first shocking lesson was learning to use the plains' most abundant source of fuel—not wood but dried buffalo dung. Smoke constantly stung the cook's eyes, and flying embers peppered her long skirt with burn holes. Wind and rain made cooking impossible at times, forcing the family into their tent or wagon to munch crackers, dried beef, and dried fruit. Wild berries, fresh meat, and fish became trail treats. "One does like a change," a woman wrote, "and about the only change we have from bread and bacon is to bacon and bread."[11] A sense of humor certainly helped.

Charlotte Pengra's journal entries kept track of her busy trail work:

> April 29, 1853 . . . made griddle cakes, stewed berries and made tea for supper. After that was over made two loaves of bread stewed pan of apples prepared potatoes and meat for breakfast, and mended a pair of pants for William pretty tired. . . . May 8 baked this morning and stewed apples this afternoon commenced washing . . . got my white clothes ready to suds. . . . I feel very tired and lonely. . . . May 14 gathered up the dishes and packed them dirty for the first time since I started. . . . May 18 washed a very large washing, unpacked dried and packed clothing—made a pair of calico cases for pillows and cooked two meals—done brave, I think.[12]

Dust coated people, animals, and possessions like a skin. Almost as thick as the dust, and more annoying, came swarms

A family with their covered wagon, Nebraska, 1886. *National Archives*

of biting fleas, mosquitoes, and gnats. For travelers with only a tent or wagon cover for protection, the unpredictable weather often proved harsh. "We have had all kinds of weather today," wrote Amelia Stewart Knight, who headed to Oregon in 1853 with her husband and seven children.[13] She continued:

> This morning was dry, dusty, and sandy. This afternoon it rained, hailed, and the wind was very high. Have been traveling all the afternoon in mud and water up to our hubs. Broke chains and stuck in the mud several times.

A few weeks later, she noted with a touch of sarcasm, "Take us all together we are a poor looking set, and all this for Oregon.

I am thinking while I write, 'Oh, Oregon, you must be a wonderful country.' Came 18 miles today."[14]

Wet weather meant soaked clothes and bedding, and every so often women hauled baggage out to air, cleaned the wagon, and repacked everything. Heavy chores like this—and the most hated chore, laundry—required a special "laying over" day when travel stopped, replaced by work and repairs.

"The Going Was Terribly Rough"

Trail life held dangers as well as discomfort and hard work. As the weeks rolled by, women hardened to shocking sights—seeing the dead lowered into graves without coffins or funerals; watching haunted people tramping home after giving up the struggle, having lost their oxen and abandoned their wagons; witnessing emigrants and animals drown as they tried crossing swollen rivers. Buffalo stampedes cost other lives. Parents worried over children. Young ones wandered off or fell and were crushed beneath wagon wheels.

The greatest threat, disease, became the emigrant's constant companion. The late 1840s and early 1850s saw a worldwide cholera epidemic, and settlers carried the disease west and spread it through feces-contaminated water supplies. Victims often died within hours, or lingered for only a few days, suffering violent diarrhea and vomiting, dehydration, and kidney failure before succumbing to the disease.

Smallpox, measles, and typhoid fever killed others; dysentery and chills and fever struck almost every traveler at some point. In June 1852 a woman observed, "All along the road up the Platte River was a grave yard; most any time of day you could see people burying their dead; some places five or six graves in a row. . . . It was a sad sight; no one can realize it unless they had seen it."[15]

Mothers turned to medicine chests filled with castor oil and camphor and drugs like belladonna and laudanum, an opium mixture. As a child in 1846, Lucy Henderson traveled west on the Oregon Trail with her family. She later recalled:

> Mother had brought some medicine along. . . . My little sister, Salita Jane wanted to taste it . . . as soon as we had gone she got the bottle and drank it all. Presently she came to the campfire where Mother was cooking supper and said she felt awfully sleepy. . . . When Mother tried to awake her later she couldn't arouse her. Lettie had drunk the whole bottle of laudanum. It was too late to save her life.[16]

Only three days after burying Lettie, Lucy's mother gave birth to a baby girl.

> We were so late that the men of the party decided we could not tarry a day, so we had to press on. The going was terribly rough. We were the first party to take the southern cut-off and there was no road. The men walked beside the wagons and tried to ease the wheels down into the rough places, but in spite of this it was a very rough ride for my mother and her new born babe.[17]

Sometime in July, wagon trains on the Oregon Trail crossed the Continental Divide at South Pass. It was a broad, flat plain that disappointed many emigrants, who expected something more spectacular. The trip was less than halfway over by this time, and the worst dangers still lay ahead. The California route to Sacramento led through sandy desert, terrible heat, and a climb over the Sierra Nevada range. Luzena Wilson described her family's hellish trek through Death Valley, a 40-mile march of scorched feet and scalding gray dust that burned their eyes red and parched their tongues. Oregon pioneers faced the Blue Mountains, the Cascade Range, and a trip down the mighty Columbia River before they reached the Willamette Valley.

By this stage of the journey, tension and fatigue marked the emigrants. Tempers flared and wagon trains sometimes splintered into smaller groups. "Our company do nothing but jaw all the time," observed one woman. "I never saw such a cross company before."[18] Taking an uncharted shortcut to save time looked tempting but could prove deadly, as the Donner Party discovered. All along the trail, furniture and tools lay abandoned to lighten the load for exhausted, bony animals. In the mountains, the struggle grew perilous. Men hoisted the wagons uphill with chains, ropes, and pulleys and then eased them down again with wheel brakes locked.

Oxen dropped dead in their tracks; the road was littered with dead cattle and bones bleached by the sun. "Shame on the man," exclaimed Amelia Stewart Knight,

> who has no pity for the poor, dumb brutes that have to travel and toil month after month on this desolate road. I could hardly help shedding tears, when we drove round this poor ox who had helped us along thus far and has given us his very last step.[19]

"We Womenfolk Visited"

Besides their jobs as trail homemakers, women helped with men's work, too. They drove wagons, pitched tents, loaded and unloaded, and yoked cattle. If her husband became ill or died, a woman managed on her own, often leaning on other females for help and emotional support. Women visited between wagons, spoke of old homes "back in the states," traded ideas to spice up the monotonous diet, and shared hopes for the future. They assisted with childbirth and comforted one another in times of loss. "Late in the afternoon," reported one journal entry, "a group of women stood watching Mrs. Wilson's little babe as it breathed its last."[20]

Another woman wrote, "The female portion of our little train are almost discouraged. We sat by moonlight and discussed matters till near 11 o'clock."[21] Exclaimed one woman, "Almira says she wished she was home, and I say ditto!"[22] Women helped out in other ways, too. On the treeless plains they might have stood in a circle, skirts fanned out, providing one another some privacy when nature called.

Months spent on the overland trails challenged every fiber of female emigrants. Breathtaking scenery and hope for the future existed alongside discomfort and despair. The trails' lessons on adapting and coping with the unexpected helped prepare women for their new lives on the frontier. Some never made it to California or Oregon, never tasted the fruits of the promised land. But others at last recorded—thankfully and with relief—in letters and diaries that the great journey had finally ended.

Margret Reed

Surviving Starvation in the Sierra Nevada

The overland trails pitted emigrants in a 2,000-mile race against winter to reach California or Oregon, and in 1846 the group known as the Donner Party lost that race. In late October, heavy snows pinned 81 exhausted people—23 men, 15 women, and 43 children, many only toddlers and infants—near Lake Truckee in the Sierra Nevada. There, the brutal weather eventually buried them beneath 30 feet of snow. Margret Reed, who'd been a young widow so frail she married her second husband, James, while lying in a sickbed, survived that winter's unspeakable horrors, and her four children survived, too.

Forty-seven-year-old James Reed in part decided to go west for the sake of Margret's health. For the long journey, the Reeds built a special wagon, with a door on the side like a carriage and bump outs over the wheels for extra room. Margret's mother, Sarah Keyes, joined the family, which included Margret's twelve-year-old daughter, Virginia, whom James had adopted, and the Reeds' little children. Among them were Patty, age eight; James Jr., age five; and Thomas, age three. They left their home in Springfield, Illinois, along with the families of George and Jacob Donner. The parties included teamsters and a few servants.

The train "jumped off" in Independence, Missouri, and joined a larger wagon train. Within days, Margret buried her mother in Kansas, a sad beginning to the adventure. The emigrants continued along the trail used by thousands of others during

Margret Reed, a drawing from a photograph made after her ordeal.
US History Images

the next decade, trudging along the Platte River and the Sweetwater River, crossing South Pass, and then making their way to the trail split where people headed into Oregon or dropped down to California.

Here, the Donner Party, urged by James Reed, opted for a third route, a supposed shorter route on an uncharted trail called the Hastings Cutoff. Others warned Reed not to risk the cutoff, but Hastings himself promised to guide the party, a pledge he broke. Nevertheless, the emigrants trudged on, hoping to make up time using a trail that didn't exist. The group included the Breen family; there were Patrick and his wife, Peggy, and their seven children. Levinah Murphy headed a clan of her children, two sons-in-law, and several little grandchildren. William and Eleanor Eddy also came, with a toddler and baby.

William McCutchen, his wife, Amanda, and their baby, Harriet, joined the Donners at Fort Bridger near the cutoff. A small group of Germans, the Kesebergs and the Wolfingers, bachelor Patrick Dolan, and hired hands completed the train. But Virginia Reed's beloved pony, Billy, having traveled all the way from Illinois, simply gave up and would not go on. As the wagons rolled off, Virginia cried herself sick, watching Billy shrink into the distance until he vanished from her sight.

In the Wasatch Mountains, they sawed and hacked their own path through a winding canyon of thick brush and trees, moving at a snail's pace. At some point, the Graves, a family of nine, traveling with three wagons, joined the Donner group in the mountains. The journey of 35 miles cost them two weeks of precious time. The party emerged near the Great Salt Lake with 600 miles still before them, "worn with travel and greatly discouraged," recalled Virginia Reed.[23]

Then they faced a great desert of seeping, boglike salt flats, where nothing bloomed. Oxen and wagons sank into the salty mire, while everyone choked on clouds of dust. They rationed water, baked in the day's heat, and shivered through the cold nights. The line of wagons stretched out as people struggled, with the Reeds near the rear of the procession.

After three days without water, the oxen stumbled, halted, and dropped to the ground. People unyoked the wagons and drove the cattle on, hoping to retrieve what they needed later. Water waited at the base of Pilot Peak, an oasis in the distance. For the Reeds, the salt flats proved a disaster. Their oxen and cattle bolted after the water, forcing the family to abandon all but one wagon and leaving them with only one ox and one cow. They had to borrow oxen to continue.

After five miserable days in the desert, the party spent a week at Pilot Peak, resting, searching for missing cattle, and bringing up some of the wagons left behind. In all, the families had lost 36 head of cattle. In a few weeks, along the Humboldt River, Indians drove off more cattle and horses. The loss of animals affected more than transportation. Without cattle, the Donner Party headed into the Sierra Nevada lacking the most precious commodity of all: potential food.

It was now late September. After so many months and so many miles, knowing they were late getting to the mountains, exhausted people vented their tempers, and tension marked every face. At one point, offering no details, James Reed simply noted, "All the women in Camp were mad with anger."[24] They reached the Humboldt River and the main trail to California two months after cleaving off onto the shortcut. They had probably lost about a month of traveling time.

Only a week later, on October 5, Margret Reed faced another heartrending challenge. As the teamsters struggled to get up a steep slope, wagons scraping, animals tangling, an argument broke out. Her husband stepped into the quarrel, and in a heated exchange, John Snyder, a teamster for the Graves family, whipped Reed about the head. Bleeding, James pulled a knife and plunged it into Snyder's chest, killing him. The shocked camp divided—had Reed committed murder or had he defended himself? Some threatened to hang James, but eventually the company decided to banish him, without food or weapons, to face death or find his way out alone.

But James refused to leave. Margret, dreading how difficult life would be without him, urged her husband to go for his own safety. Yet how could he abandon his family, even for a while? Think of the children, Margret reminded him. They were nearly destitute, and if he could bring back supplies, he might save them all.

James and Margret struggled with the awful decision. In the end, he left, after others promised they would help his wife and children. Margret watched him go, not knowing if she'd ever see her husband again. Virginia stole after her father into the darkness and brought him his rifle.

At first, Margret nearly gave way to despair. Virginia and Patty actually feared for her life. But the tormenting knowledge that her children faced danger and starvation released new reserves of energy. With 400 miles to go, Margret and her children would deal with whatever came. They lived on small food rations, and soon Margret abandoned their remaining wagon—it was just too heavy for the exhausted, skeletal oxen to pull. They packed what they could into another emigrant's wagon, carried some, and left the rest. Margret and the girls walked while the small boys rode the family's two starved horses. After 40 miles of desert, heat, and thirst, with their animals staggering and more oxen dying along the way, the company finally hit the Truckee River—an oasis of green and fresh water—and followed the river into the mountains.

On October 19, Charles Stanton, who'd left in mid-September with William McCutchen to seek help at Sutter's Fort in California, met up with the emigrants. He led seven mules loaded with supplies and brought two Indian guides—a glad sight for the Donner Party. Even better for the Reeds, he'd seen James, famished but alive and well on the trail. With only 100 miles to go and a new supply of food and men to guide them, everyone must have felt the worst of the journey had ended.

The families spread out, some pushing hard to the front, the Donners straggling behind. On October 31, those in the front reached Lake Truckee, softly blanketed in snow, and viewed the steep climb that awaited. The next day Stanton and the two Indians led Margret and her children, the Eddys, and the Graves family toward the summit. Others stayed below at the lake, too exhausted to attempt the mountain.

The farther they climbed, the deeper the snow became. People and animals lurched through the drifts. The party abandoned their wagons and lashed belongings to the oxen. Stanton and one of the Indians scouted ahead to the summit before tracking back to urge the climbers on for the final push. But the emigrants had built fires on the snow; worn out, they huddled close to the flames. Stanton promised that if no more snow fell they could reach the pass—they had only about three miles to go, but no one had the heart to leave the fires. They'd forge ahead at dawn.

During the night, a storm howled over the mountains, and snow nearly buried the unsheltered emigrants. Margret blanketed her children with shawls and roused herself from sleep every few minutes to brush off the drifting white flakes. By morning, mountain and valley lay deep in snow, and everyone realized there was no way now they'd reach the summit. "With heavy hearts," wrote Virginia Reed, the company stumbled back down to the lake.

The Breens occupied a cabin that had been built and abandoned several years before. Men chopped and hewed trees and built two more cabins, covering the roofs with hides. The Murphys took one, and Margret and her children shared a divided cabin with the Graves family. The Eddys bunked with the Murphys. William's wife, Amanda McCutchen, and her baby stayed with the Graveses. Stanton and the Indians stayed with the Reeds. Keseberg built a lean-to against the Breen's cabin. The Donners, who'd lagged behind due to a wagon accident, made it as far as Alder Creek, about seven miles from the lake cabins. They had no time to build a wooden shelter and would spend the winter in tents with brush and tree boughs for protection.

Most of the remaining cattle were killed and buried in the snow. Margret Reed possessed no cattle, but she bartered for some by promising to give two cows for one when they finally reached California. Franklin Graves and Patrick Breen each gave her two animals, but the poor creatures, so weak and starved after walking 2,000 miles, provided little meat. Tired, already half starved themselves, people hunkered down. All Midwesterners, they had no idea of winter's fury on the mountains. The first storm lasted for eight days.

On November 12, about 15 people tried to break out and make it over the mountain, but the snow forced them back. A second attempt a week later also ended in failure. Another storm raged over the camp in late November, continuing into the first days of December. The remaining cattle and horses vanished in the storm, probably buried beneath the deep drifts, leaving the emigrants with no way to find the carcasses.

The cabins shrank as the snow piled up, and few people had the energy or the will to move about. Collecting firewood became monumental work. Looking at one another, the emigrants could clearly see each other's gaunt faces and bony ribs and shoulders—their families and companions were dwindling away.

A month in, Franklin Graves proposed they try again—someone had to get through and bring back food and help. They fashioned snowshoes, and the healthiest adults and teens attempted the climb. Two people had already perished in camp when the group of seventeen (ten men, five women, and two of the Murphy boys, ages thirteen and ten) started out. Several were young parents who left their children behind with the others, seeing no way to save their little ones but to get help.

Margret and the others could only wait and hope. Unprotected from the elements, the snowshoers suffered biting cold, heavy snowstorms and howling winds, wet clothes, and tiny rations of food—until no food remained at all. One by one, they perished, until the survivors resorted to the only thing they could to stay alive—they became the first of the Donner Party to cut away strips of flesh from their dead companions and eat them to stave off starvation.

Finally, seven survivors, two men and all five women, stumbled into a Miwok Indian village, where they received food. When no one else could go on, William Eddy summoned the will to advance. A month after they'd left the lake, he staggered upon a place called Johnson's Ranch on January 17 and found help. But how would they get help back to those who waited?

At the lake and at Alder Creek, no one knew the fate of the snowshoers. Milt Elliot, a teamster, staggered over to the cabins from Alder Creek with the sad news that Jacob Donner had died, as had three of the young, single men with the party. Such news only added to the sense of desperation and hopelessness.

Margret did her best to revive a few hours of Christmas joy for her hungry children. She'd saved a meager hoard for the occasion—a few dried apples, a few beans, a little tripe, and a small piece of bacon. The children watched as the treats simmered in the kettle, and when they sat down to this Christmas feast, Margret told them, "Children, eat slowly, for this one day you can have all you wish." For the rest of her life, no matter how grand a Christmas dinner spread on her table, Virginia never forgot what her mother did for them. "So bitter was the misery relieved by that one bright day, that I have never since sat down to a Christmas dinner without my thoughts going back to Donner Lake."[25]

They lived in crowded, dark cabins beneath the snow, lice and vermin an added source of misery. People could scarcely walk; they dragged themselves between cabins. When the men did cut trees for fuel, the heavy logs fell deep down into the snow and had to be wrestled out. When the snow fell too deep, they chipped bits of wood off cabin walls to burn for warmth. Children cried with hunger, and mothers cried because they had no food to give their little ones.

Margret, along with the others, cut cowhide into strips, singed off the hair, and then boiled the leather into a gelatinous gruel. She traded the only valuable items she still had, James's watch and his Masonic medal, for food. But when she had nothing left to barter and no hopes, she decided that she would try again to get over the mountain, accompanied by Virginia and her two employees, Milt Elliot and Eliza Williams. She begged people to take in Patty, James, and Thomas—they were too small to attempt the mountain. But no one wanted more mouths to feed. Finally, she persuaded the Graveses to take James, while Patty and Thomas went to the Breens' cabin. Margret ripped herself from her crying children with promises she'd bring them back bread.

They started out the morning of January 4. But after five days in the mountains, with Virginia so weak she often crawled, and her feet nearly frozen, Margret decided they must turn back.

By the time they returned, the cowhide that had served as their roof was gone, and the Reeds had no place to live. The Breens allowed Margret and her four children to stay with them. For Margret, though discouraged, it was enough just to have the family united once again. Peggy Breen, against her husband's wishes, sometimes slipped small bits of food to the Reed children. At one point, sure that Virginia lay near death, Peggy took Margret outside into the snow and warned her to prepare for her daughter's passing. But Virginia survived.

On January 22, another blizzard struck, bringing whiteout snows and screaming, pitiless winds that prevented sleep. After the travelers had been trapped for three and a half months, February brought deaths in quick succession. The living dragged the bodies outside and covered them with snow. People boiled cow bones. Margret had nothing, and those with small amounts of food understandably hoarded them for their own families. No one could survive much longer without help.

Yet they had not been forgotten. James Reed and William McCutchen had tried to get over the mountain in the fall but had been driven back by storms. They began a frantic wait to reach their families. Now, in February, money had been raised, and several rescue parties had gathered, with animals and food prepared and loaded. But storms and deep snow hampered the rescuers just as the merciless winter held the emigrants captive.

On February 18, the first relief party reached the lake, seeing no signs of life. But slowly, thin voices answered their calls, and faces began appearing out of the snow. The rescuers handed out jerked beef and biscuits. The next morning several trudged on to the Donner tents, where conditions were even worse than at the cabins.

An attempt had to be made to get out that very day; they could not delay. Again, families decided who should go and who should stay and await help. The rescuers evaded questions about the snowshoe group that had left months before. It was no use demoralizing starving people who now faced climbing over the mountains. The rescuers divided up what provisions they'd brought, chopped some firewood, and prepared to leave. No one knew if another storm would rage over the mountains and dash all their hopes.

Margret determined that she and all four of her children must go. The first relief set off with 23 skeleton-thin emigrants, most of them under the age of 14, including three three-year-olds who had to be carried. Once they were trudging up the mountain it became clear that little Patty Reed and Thomas Reed would not be able to go on. Reason Tucker, one of the leaders of the first rescue party, told Margret the children must go back, but he promised to see that they safely reached the lake cabins.

Margret refused, saying she would return to camp with the little ones and leave Virginia and James to continue the escape. Tucker quietly pointed out that the camp didn't need another adult mouth to feed, and Virginia and James needed her help to get over the mountain. She must leave Patty and Thomas behind.

In anguish, Margret debated what was best and then asked Tucker if he was a Mason like her husband. He was, and she asked him to vow as a Mason that he'd make sure her children were cared for. If Margret's heart had not already broken as she knelt to part with Patty and Thomas, it must have shattered as Patty said, "Well, Ma, if you never see me again, do the best you can."[26] Virginia remembered her sister telling Margret, "I want to see papa, but I will take good care of Tommy and I do not want you to come back."[27]

Men turned away to hide their tears as Margret said good-bye to her children. Below at the lake, no one wanted the

Reed children, but Tucker convinced the Breens to take them in, helped in part by promises that more rescuers and supplies were on the way. He did not know this for sure, but the promise worked.

The trudge up the mountain continued; the party struggled, climbing out of snow and then sinking in again. Five-year-old James Reed, too big to be carried, worked extra hard, proclaiming every step took him closer to his father and food. Wet, then frozen, but always hungry, the group boiled the hems of buckskin pants and shoelaces.

Some of the rescuers pushed ahead, hoping to meet help—and they did. James Reed and his relief party ran into the first relief and eventually came upon the strung-out line of emigrants, holding out bony hands and pleading for bread. Someone shouted to Margret that her husband had come. She fell to her knees in joy while Virginia plunged, falling and lumbering, into her father's arms. It was February 27.

But the happy reunion lasted only minutes. Margret told James that Patty and Thomas remained at the lake; he must go quickly and bring them out. So while Margret, Virginia, and little James continued west, James headed toward the camp, hoping to find his two children still alive.

On March 7, Margret, Virginia, and James reached Johnson's Ranch to find grass and even wildflowers. It seemed like paradise to the children, but Margret ached with worry for her husband, for Patty and Thomas. She stood in the cabin doorway for hours, looking up at the mountain, hoping to see signs of them, not knowing that more unspeakable horrors faced her loved ones.

James arrived at the cabins to find Patty and Thomas still alive. The rescuers clearly saw that people had survived by eating the dead, for half-butchered bodies lay about on the ground.

The rescuers made soup with the provisions they'd lugged in, and Patty baked bread with the precious flour. They must leave camp the following day. Again, people agonized—who had strength to leave, who would send their children on, who would stay with the weak and dying. Seventeen people left camp with James Reed's rescue team, including the Breen family and the remaining family of Elizabeth Graves. Others remained at the lake.

By the third day, the party had reached a high crest of the mountain. Exposed completely to the elements, people cried with cold and ached for food. As gray clouds thickened, James Reed wrote in his journal, "Terror, terror." By night, the snow came, blowing sideways and howling, pelting them with ice. People wept and prayed. The snow blinded James. They kept a fire going. Daylight brought no relief—the storm raged on. The fire sank slowly into the snow. "Hunger, hunger is the Cry with the Children and nothing to give them," wrote James, "Freesing was the Cry of the mothers with reference to their little starving freesing Children."[28] Safely at Johnson's Ranch, Margret knew a storm raged in the mountains and felt sick with fear for her family.

Before the storm abated, James lay near death, but he recovered enough to go on. As James prepared to leave, others simply lay in a state of collapse. A Donner child had died; Elizabeth Graves was nearly dead. Reed argued and urged them on. He then called another man to witness that he'd done the best he could—he had not abandoned them. The rescuers stacked up a three-day supply of wood for the 13 people who stayed on the mountain, and they left with only three children from the camp—Patty, Thomas, and Solomon Hook, Jacob Donner's stepson.

Again suffering from snow blindness, James kept his little party staggering on. When Patty faltered, he tied her to his back with a blanket. Fellow rescuer Hiram Miller carried Thomas and helped James up when he fell. Fearing for Patty's life, James fed her scrapings of meat he'd saved in the thumb of his mitten.

With great relief they met another rescue effort coming toward them and carrying food for empty bellies. Reed told them of the others stranded on the mountain. The third relief found 11 survivors; they'd lived by eating the dead. This rescue included William Eddy and William Foster, who'd survived the ordeal of the snowshoe escape. Sadly, they arrived too late at the lake camp to save their own little children. By April, the last survivor had been rescued. Thirty-six people had died; 45 had survived. Death spared only two families, the Breens and the Reeds. Margret had somehow kept her brood alive, and Virginia noted they were the only family that had lived without eating human flesh.

The story of the Donner Party became a sensation, with reporters embellishing the more gruesome details as the months and years passed. At the time, many acknowledged openly what they'd done to survive. Other people, at other times and places, have done the same. They were ordinary men and women, families with children, trapped in horrendous circumstances. A few survivors later denied they'd turned to cannibalism. Recent excavations have found no evidence of human bones among the boiled bone fragments. But the emigrants most likely did not boil the bones of the dead; they sliced what they needed from the bodies and left them.

From the safety and warmth of California in summer, Virginia wrote her cousin in Illinois. She had not written half of what they'd suffered, she said—how could she even describe it? But she offered a few words of wisdom: "Never take no cutoffs and hury along as fast as you can."[29]

Margret never enjoyed the robust health she'd hoped for in the West. She died in 1861 at age 47, knowing her children and grandchildren prospered, far from the icy shadows of Truckee Lake. The Donner Party's story magnified every danger of the overland trail to extremes. The fact that so many lived stands as a testament to the human spirit of survival.

Amelia Stewart Knight

On the Oregon Trail

On April 9, 1853, Amelia Stewart Knight, her husband Joel, and seven children—Plutarch, Seneca, Frances, Jefferson, Lucy, Almira, and Chatfield—left their home in Iowa for the Oregon Territory. For the next five months, Amelia kept a steady diary of their journey, and because a lady did not discuss such things openly, never once does she mention she faced this great adventure pregnant, once again.

Rain and cold marked the early days of the expedition as they crept along "out of one mud hole into another all day."[30] Facing life with only a tent or wagon cover for protection became a depressing

Amelia Stewart Knight.
Oregon Historical Society

obstacle of the journey. Late April storms blew down tents and capsized a few wagons. A few days after they began, they met their first Indians. "Lucy and Almira afraid and run into the wagon to hide," Amelia reported. Soon, though, the children grew used to the Indians who often camped around the settlers, "begging money and something to eat."

The journey cost money. The family paid up to eight dollars per wagon to be ferried across rivers whenever possible. They also shelled out cash at times for corn or hay to feed their livestock. Amelia worried over the health of each horse, milk cow, and ox, animals needed not only to sustain them for the trip, but to help establish the family in the Oregon Territory.

On May 5, the family joined another company of emigrants, swelling their party to 24 men and granting Amelia peace of mind with more protection. The next day they passed a train of wagons plodding back east. The head man had drowned a few days before while getting his cattle across the Elkhorn River. "With sadness and pity I passed those who perhaps a few days before had been well and happy as ourselves," Amelia wrote.

River crossings clogged the trail—Amelia counted more than 300 other wagons waiting with them to cross the Elkhorn. At this spot, without a ferry, the family unloaded the wagons to shuttle their goods across in the tightest wagon bed a little at a time. With a long rope stretched across the river, men pulled everything to the opposite shore. The wagons themselves were broken down, carried over, and put back together, an incredible amount of work. "Women and children were taken last, and then swim the cattle and horses." The family faced many river crossings on the long journey west, each one a descent into danger for people and animals.

Violent storms battered the wagon train through May, often preventing them from building a fire or pitching the tents. On those nights the family retired to bed with empty stomachs, sleeping the best they could in their soaked clothes. "I never saw such a storm," Amelia penned on May 17. "The wind was so high I thought it would tear the wagons to pieces . . . in less than 2 hours the water was a foot deep all over our camp grounds." A fearful display of crackling lightning killed several cows. At the end of May, the wagon train came upon a group of men skinning a buffalo, the first buffalo they'd encountered, and though only a carcass, the animal caused some excitement. "We got a mess and cooked some for supper," Amelia wrote, "very good and tender."

At times, the crowded trail seemed to stretch ahead of them forever, a long line of wagons and cattle. May 31 brought a bit of excitement when they found themselves tangled up with two large herds (called droves) of cattle and 50 wagons. "We either had to stay poking behind them in the dust or hurry up and drive past them," Amelia explained. "It was no fool of a job to be mixed up with several hundred head of cattle, and only one road to travel in, and the drovers threatening to drive their cattle over you if you attempted to pass them. They even took out their pistols." Amelia's party steered off the road and went at a trot around the drovers, wagons, and cows. "I had rather a rough ride to be sure, but was glad to get away from such a lawless set. . . . We left some swearing men behind us," she noted.

In early June, the party passed Fort Laramie and found themselves surrounded by Lakota Indians anxious to trade beads and moccasins for bread. They faced scorching heat, in the upper 90s. Amelia recorded that there was "not a drop of water, nor a spear of grass to be seen, nothing but barren hills, bare and broken rocks, sand and dust." In one incident the oxen became so "crazy for water" that they charged down into the Platte River still wearing their yokes. The family "had a great deal of trouble to keep the stock from drinking [alkaline water]. . . . It is almost sure to kill man or beast who drink it."

A new villain, swarms of biting mosquitoes, joined the party. They made life even more miserable. Mountain snows brought some water relief but soon gave way to sandy desert, and Amelia fed handfuls of flour to the hungry oxen pulling the wagons.

On July 9, they reached the forks of the emigrant road, and Amelia hoped grazing would improve "as most of the large trains are bound for California." As the thermometer climbed past 100 degrees, the heat sometimes proved too much for her, and she could barely crawl out of the wagon in the mornings to throw breakfast together. The stench along the road also sickened Amelia, an effect heightened by her advancing pregnancy; the smell of death, from cattle "lying in every direction," hung like a foul blanket over the trail. "We are still traveling on in search of water, water," she wrote in late July.

As July passed into August, each day like another, Amelia noted, "The roads have been very dusty, no water, nothing but dust and dead cattle all the day, the air is filled with the odor from cattle." Some days they traveled for 20 miles without water.

Caring for her children under such conditions proved difficult, especially as she entered the last months of her pregnancy and exhaustion took its toll. Two-year-old Chat caused the most concern. She nursed him through a fever, caused by mosquito bites, Amelia believed. Then she nursed the gravely ill toddler through scarlet fever. Lucy and Almira suffered a miserable bout of poison ivy on their legs.

Twice Chat fell out of the wagon, and once he barely missed being run over by one of the tall wheels. Amelia wrote in her diary, "I never was so much frightened in my life." In another scary incident, the family left Lucy behind—distracted, she'd been watching wagons cross a river and hadn't noticed that her parents' party had moved on. Miles later, when the company stopped to rest, another wagon train arrived with a very frightened Lucy in tow. Amelia was horrified when she discovered what had happened. She had assumed Lucy was riding in a friend's wagon, and the friend had been told that Lucy was with her mother—so no one had missed the girl. The narrow escape shocked Amelia. "It was a lesson to all of us," she wrote.

On July 25, a calf and one of their best milk cows died, a financial blow to the family and a personal loss for Amelia. "Presumed they were both poisoned with water or weeds," she noted. "Left our poor cow for the wolves and started on." August proved deadly for the cattle: another cow died, an ox drowned, and another ox dropped dead on the road, worn out with labor, heat, thirst, and lack of good grazing.

At the ferry for the Snake River, they found a unique service—Native Americans, for a fee, would swim the horses and cattle across, a job the Knights thankfully paid for. The Indians they met there "seemed peaceful and friendly." The family bought salmon—the first they'd ever tasted—from Indian fishermen. Further along the trail, after searching in vain for fresh water, they ran into a group of Cayuse Indians who showed them the way to a spring. They also purchased a few potatoes, "which will be a treat for our supper," noted Amelia.

By mid-August, the going was rough. Swift rivers tumbled over rocks, and mountains loomed. Heat gave way to frost, and water buckets froze over by morning. On September 6, they camped near the foot of the Cascade Mountains and prepared to cross, throwing away items and burning most of the deck boards on the wagons to lighten the load. Amelia washed clothes, exhausting herself to the point of illness.

The wagons crept up the steep, rough, and rocky road, twisting around holes and fallen trees. A primordial darkness settled over the trail as trees rose 300 feet into the air, blocking out much of the natural light. Yokes, chains, whole wagons, dead horses, oxen, mules, and cows littered the road. On Saturday, September 10, Amelia wrote simply, "It would be useless for me with my pencil to describe the awful road we have just passed over." Large with child, she spent most of the day staggering through the trees alongside the narrow road, tripping and climbing over logs, often carrying two-year-old Chat in her arms. "I was sick all night," she records, "and not able to get out of the wagon in the morning."

They stopped to rest at a farm, paid dearly for food, and prepared to travel again toward "some place we don't know where." A few days after September 17, Amelia gave birth to her eighth child, a boy they named Wilson. With a baby in her arms, she spent three harrowing days traveling with the rest of the family down the rushing Columbia River, using a skiff, canoes, and a flatboat. They arrived at their destination, greeted by rain, mud, and gloom. Food prices were "all too dear for poor folks," she wrote (eggs cost one dollar a dozen), "so we have treated ourselves to some small turnips at the rate of 25 cents per dozen."

Her husband traded two yoke of oxen for a half section of land (with half an acre already planted in potatoes) and a small, windowless log cabin. So, at last, after five months from Iowa to near Milwaukie, Oregon Territory, with her family's future but a blank canvas, Amelia Knight again wrote in her diary, signing off, "This is the journey's end."

2

OH, GIVE ME A HOME

"I made a great effort to be comfortable upon very little, and simply had to do it."[1]

—Frances Grummond, army wife, 1866

Outside Sacramento, California, Luzena Wilson's wagon party met a man dressed in a clean white shirt. Luzena had not seen a clean white shirt for four months and now noted her own appearance with embarrassment. A ragged bonnet shaded her sunburned face. Her skirt bottom had worn to rags, showing her ankles, while the sleeves at her elbows hung in tatters. Without gloves, her hands had grown brown and hardened. The soles of her leather shoes flapped unattached to the uppers. Thus clad in raggedy splendor, the Wilson family arrived at their new California home.

After months on the overland trails, many settlers arrived in Oregon and California poor, ragged, thin, and sometimes disheartened, with little more than relief that they had survived the trip. "People say they would not have staid they would go right back," wrote Martha Morrison Minto in 1844. "I would like to know how we could go back . . . we had no horses, nor cattle, nor anything to haul us across the plains; we had no provisions; we could not start out naked and destitute in every way."[2]

Lucky travelers found families who had come before willing to rent them space until spring. Others continued housekeeping in wagons and tents, longing for real homes. At the very least, they wanted a roof overhead and a solid floor beneath their feet. Some people dug out hillsides and burrowed in, furniture and all, until better shelter could be built. In mining camps, flimsy shacks covered in tar paper sprang up overnight. Other primitive first homes included a hollow tree stump, a cave of hay bales, and an old corncrib.

Rough conditions ruled. Pioneers who'd abandoned so much on the trails arrived with few essential items to begin home life. One woman counted her possessions as a kettle, three knives, and two sheets. Another woman, who worked at a boardinghouse in California, complained of ankle-deep mud and described:

> All the kitchen that I have is 4 posts stuck into the ground and covered over the top with factory cloth no floor but the ground. . . . I am scareing the Hogs out of my kitchen and Driving the mules out of my Dining room.[3]

Homesickness permeated the early months of settlement: "i wish I was home I would give all the gold in California," lamented one woman, "i am so homesick I do not know what to do."[4] Life appeared different and harsh. Wrote Miriam Colt, "I have cooked so much out in the hot sun and smoke that I hardly know who I am, and when I look in the little looking glass I ask, 'Can this be me?'"[5]

But despite crude conditions, many women remained hopeful. "I did not like it very well," admitted one, "but after we have taken our claim and became settled once more I began to like it much better and the longer I live here the better I like it."[6]

In western areas with plentiful trees, a log cabin became the first permanent home of many settlers. Early cabins, usually only one room, lacked glass windows or a wooden floor. Stones or sticks mashed together with clay built the fireplace chimneys and again served as chinking, packed in the spaces between the logs.

It wasn't long, however, before the elements dried and shrank the chinking, allowing hot, dusty air to whistle through cracks in summer, followed by icy blasts in winter. A South Dakota woman complained that her log house "needed repair all the time" and solved the insulation problem by surrounding her home with piles of manure in the fall to keep it snug for winter. "When the smell got bad in the spring," she noted, "we knew it was time to take the insulation away."[7] After the first year's crop had sold, or the family business nurtured along, lofts, lean-tos, floors and window glass, as well an extra room or two, could be added.

Home on the Plains

From North Dakota down to Texas, the western plains wore a desolate and lonely face—open, arid, scoured by the wind. But the land early pioneers avoided grew more attractive with passage of the Homestead Act in 1862. The act allowed the head of

The Chrisman sisters, homesteaders in Custer County, Nebraska, outside a sod house, 1886. *Nebraska State Historical Society*

a household to pay a small filing fee on a 160-acre claim at a government land office. If the family lived on the claim and farmed it for five years, the land was theirs. Many men—but also some single and widowed women—took up the challenge.

Women living on the Great Plains learned quickly what sort of house they'd now call home—one with no bricks, no wooden planks or logs. They had undertaken the mighty journey and left real homes behind for one-room houses made of dirt. One girl recalled her overwhelmed mother's reaction:

> When our covered wagon drew up beside the door of the one-roomed sod house that father had provided, he helped mother down and I remember how her face

looked as she gazed about that barren farm, then threw her arms about his neck and gave way to the only fit of weeping I ever remember seeing her indulge in.[8]

Earth was the only real building material available in many parts of the plains. A sharp shovel cut sod bricks into strips about one foot wide, two feet long, and four inches thick. Each brick weighed about 50 pounds. They were stacked, grassy side down, to form the one-room house. Boards laid over door and window openings supported more sod piled on top. Loose dirt and mud filled in between the bricks. Overhead, a frame of poles covered with brush and more sod made a roof, while people trod a floor of packed-down earth underfoot.

These "soddies" offered protection and insulation against heat and cold, and they wouldn't burn during a deadly prairie fire. But the houses' damp mustiness was inescapable, and cleaning the dwellings seemed a fool's work—how did you keep a dirt house clean? In rainstorms, the soddies dripped and ran with mud. Women tried tacking up yards of muslin to catch constant sprinklings of dirt from the walls and ceilings that drifted over furniture, food, and people. Mice, bugs, and snakes felt perfectly at home in these houses made of dirt. One girl remembered from her pioneering childhood,

> Sometimes the bull snakes would get in the roof and now and then one would lose his hold and fall down on the bed, and then off on the floor. Mother would grab the hoe and there was something doing and after the fight was over Mr. Bull Snake was dragged outside.[9]

Railroad companies owned vast tracts of Western land and tempted settlers with advertisements promising, "Land for the

Plains weather often arrived in extremes, much like this dust storm over Midland, Texas, 1894. *National Archives*

Landless!" and "Homes for the Homeless!" Europeans arrived in the tens of thousands, each willing to face the risks for a chance to own land.

Former slaves, freed after the Civil War, came too. Some established all-black communities like those in Nicodemus, Kansas, and Boley, Oklahoma. "In the earliest days," recalled an African American pioneer woman, "each family was grateful for the help of each other family and 'we were all on a level.' However, later differences arose and sentiment against Negros developed."[10] Discrimination was not the only problem facing African American settlers. The plains proved a brutal challenge in themselves.

An African American family in Nicodemus, Kansas.
www.legendsofamerica.com

Weather often arrived in extremes: withering heat, drought, wind and dust storms, downpours, hail, cyclones, bitter cold, and blizzards dumping drifts 40 feet deep. Invasions of mosquitoes, bedbugs, lice, and grasshoppers plagued families. For fuel, women continued burning dried buffalo chips or cow dung, or they gathered dried tumbleweed or twisted the tough prairie grass into sticks. Water for chores, drinking, and cooking proved in short supply. Women helped dig wells, melted snow, reused water for several tasks, and lugged it long distances from creeks or streams.

The lack of trees made life on the plains even more harsh and lonely. One woman, accompanying her husband to a distant stream to collect wood, threw her arms around a tree trunk and wept at her first sight of a tree in two years. Elizabeth Custer followed her soldier-husband General George Custer around the West and described the hardships in a land of constant glare and little shade. Nebraska author Willa Cather (1873–1947) wrote:

> Trees were so rare in that country, and they had to make such a hard fight to grow, that we used to feel anxious about them, and visit them as if they were persons. It must have been the scarcity of detail in that tawny landscape that made detail so precious.[11]

The plains defeated some families, who gave up and retreated east. Others hung on, finding solace in sarcastic songs such as this Kansas ditty:

Ada McColl collecting chips in Kansas, 1893. *Kansas State Historical Society*

But Hurrah for Lane County, the land of the free
The home of the grasshopper, bedbug, and flea
I'll sing her loud praises and boast of her fame
While starving to death on my government claim.[12]

However uninviting, Western lands meant financial security to many people. Both women and men put up with hard work and disasters for the mere hope of a better future. By 1910, at least 10 percent of plains homesteaders were single women. Some, divorced or widowed, had children to support. Others had never married and trekked west seeking adventure and the freedom to earn their own living.

"It Does Not Look Much Like Home"

In all corners of the West, the main job of any woman was preparing a home and caring for her family. With little to work with, Western women set to their task, creating homes from adobe bricks (a mixture of clay and straw), tar paper, sod, and logs. Wrote one Kansas woman,

> The wind whistled through the walls in winter and dust blew in summer, but we papered the walls with newspapers and made rag carpets for the floors, and thought we were living well, very enthusiastic over the new country we intended to conquer.[13]

Homey touches made all the difference, even in a dirt house. A stack of books, colorful quilts spread over beds, or a prized musical instrument placed in a position of honor created the feeling of home. One woman insisted her family sit outdoors for a photographer, all of them posed around her ornate organ. She refused to have her sod house appear in the background!

Curtains seemed of special value in creating a civilized home, and some women sacrificed wedding dresses or fancy petticoats for the cause. Women lined packing crates with calico cloth to make dish cupboards. Wildflowers in crocks and pitchers graced tables, and geraniums coaxed to bloom on windowsills uplifted spirits. As Laura Ingalls Wilder remembered from the many moves of her pioneering childhood, when Ma's red-and-white-checked tablecloth decked the table and her china shepherdess smiled from a special bracket Pa had made, the Ingalls family always knew they were home.

Most places were small, poor, and cheap, but as one woman proclaimed, a two-room, tar-papered shack could seem like a palace. "For was it not my home," she asked, "after six months spent in an ox wagon?"[14] Later, some Western homes rivaled houses east of the Missouri River in style and comfort: frame farmhouses, Victorian homes with all the fancy trimmings, and the grand mansions of mine owners.

Army Life

While most women strived to set down roots, army wives faced the hassle of constant transfers from fort to fort. As a new bride, Elizabeth Custer wrote to her husband, George, "I had rather live in a tent, outdoors with you than in a palace with another. There is no place I would not go to, gladly, live in gladly, because . . . I love you."[15]

Mrs. Custer lived in army forts from North Dakota to Texas during her 12-year marriage. Newlywed Frances Roe cried herself sick on learning of another move. She resented leaving behind her belongings and a cherished pet dog. Often army families could not afford to cart all of their household possessions to their next posts. Other women helped out, buying friends' dishes and other goods that there was no room to pack. Confided Elizabeth Custer to a friend:

> Had I ever had any housekeeping desires they would long have been quenched, so frequently do we move. What things we retain from our many moving are put down in quarters never in remarkable repair.[16]

Army houses ranged from tents to drafty, leaky, cramped structures, infested with pests like ants and rattlesnakes. Like other Western wives, army women set to work improving the comfort of their homes with what little they had. Any items needed to spruce up their quarters, even a yard of canvas, had to be supplied by the post quartermaster, a typically stingy man

Elizabeth Custer with George, her husband (seated), and Tom Custer, her brother-in-law, around 1866. Elizabeth authored three books about her army life in the West. Both men died at the Battle of the Little Bighorn, June 25, 1876. *Library of Congress*

who "controlled all supplies, and could make us either comfortable or the reverse, as he chose," explained Frances Boyd.[17]

But just when quarters seemed homelike, an army wife might face the perils of "ranking out." When a new officer arrived at a fort, he claimed the best quarters his rank allowed, forcing officers of lower rank into other housing. Frances Boyd, stationed in New Mexico with her husband and three little children, was bumped from a four-room house into one room by the arrival of an unmarried captain. While the captain generously allowed the Boyds a four-week grace period because the children were ill, another army wife had only three hours to vacate her home.

As an added insult, an officer's low pay had to cover food, travel, moving expenses, and other necessities. With eggs (when available) selling for two dollars a dozen at the fort's supply store, butter for $2.50 a pound, and kerosene fuel at five dollars a gallon, army families remained poor and hungry. Fresh fruit, vegetables, and dairy were nearly unheard of. "The cookbooks were maddening to us," wrote Elizabeth Custer, "for a casual glance at any of them proves how necessary eggs, butter, and cream are to every recipe."[18] The Boyds existed on bacon, beans, flour, rice, coffee, tea, and sugar, with dried apples as a treat.

There were officers who felt a woman had no business on the military scene, and some enlisted men disliked the extra work required when a woman traveled with the regiment. The women tried hard not to burden anyone, and Elizabeth Custer claimed proudly that she could bathe and dress in seven minutes and be ready to march. Frances Boyd, while traveling in New Mexico, recalled her greatest praise came from a captain who said she'd "never caused one moment's delay or trouble."[19]

But officers' wives resented military regulations and protocols that ignored them completely. Elizabeth Custer complained that the regulation book went into great detail about every little thing, even the number of hours that bean soup should boil, so that "it would be natural to suppose that a paragraph or two might be wasted on an officer's wife!"[20] What really riled the well-bred, educated women married to officers was the fact that the army looked upon them as camp followers, the same as laundresses, or worse, prostitutes. The strict military separation between an officer and his men carried over to the army wives, and an officer's lady did not socialize with an enlisted man's wife or a company laundress.

All military wives shared the same fears for their husbands' and their families' safety in the Western wilds. They often lived in "hostile" country surrounded by Native Americans fighting to keep their homelands. Though the army wife watched her husband march out to heroic tunes and the sentimental strains of "The Girl I Left Behind Me," Elizabeth Custer noted that "no expedition goes out with shout and song, if loving, weeping women are left behind."[21]

"Very Little Female Society"

Most women, especially during the early months of pioneering, missed female companionship. Many echoed Frances Grummond's joy at learning four other women lived at her new army fort: "Here we were again among women. . . . Hope sprang up!"[22] A rancher's wife described her California home as beautiful but lonely. "We are miles from our nearest neighbor," she wrote, "and they only men. I was alone with my children most of the time for the first four months, my husband being away attending to business interests."[23] Another woman welcomed the railroad reaching into her area, connecting her with the life and family she had known before she went west.

Sometimes months passed between visits with another woman—a white woman, that is. Native American women lived throughout the American West, and Mexican and Spanish women had lived in the Southwest for over a century. But white women, carting old prejudices and fears to the frontier, were not always ready to befriend the women who already called the West home.

For many hardworking women, the lack of females in their new Western homes blossomed into economic opportunity. In the California mining camps especially, women's skills flourished under a wave of high demand. As one California pioneer excitedly planned, "A woman that can work will make more money than a man, and I think now that I shall do that."[24]

Narcissa Whitman

Alone, in the Thick Darkness of Heathendom

When new bride Narcissa Whitman began the grueling overland journey on an old Indian path that would soon be known as the Oregon Trail, she barely knew her husband, Marcus. She'd pushed the limits of old-maid-hood by not marrying until the ripe old age of 28. The two agreed to marriage without courtship or romance. Instead, a passion for missionary work forged the bond between Narcissa and Marcus.

Although well-educated, with experience as a teacher and a leading participant in her upstate New York church, Narcissa faced difficulties gaining acceptance from the American Board of Commissioners for Foreign Missions (ABCFM) without a "missionary husband." Marcus, too, had been discouraged by the board; they'd encouraged him to wed a "missionary wife." A wife could teach natives to read and write; and a missionary family served as a model for the natives. Missionary men needed helpmates, "well-educated and pious females who have formed all their habits and modes of thinking in a Christian country." And of course, wives insured male missionaries remained happy and productive. The sight of a wife and children served as a symbol of peace, "well understood and appreciated by savages."[25]

The ABCFM decided Narcissa and Marcus should establish their mission among the American Indians of Oregon. Several Western tribes, including the Nez Percé, had expressed interest in learning about Christianity. Marcus had traveled west already, and he believed a woman could successfully make the long journey. He'd worked to recruit others to join him in his mission to the Northwest. Henry Spalding, whose marriage proposal Narcissa had once rejected, and his wife, Eliza, would travel with the Whitmans. The two women would be the first females to journey across the continent.

At their wedding on February 18, 1836, the day before departing for Oregon, Narcissa sang a missionary hymn that left the guests sobbing into their handkerchiefs.

In the deserts let me labor,
On the mountains let me tell,
How he died—the blessed Saviour—
To redeem a world from hell!
Let me hasten, let me hasten,
Far in heathen lands to dwell.

The journey from New York to Saint Louis seemed an idyllic honeymoon to Narcissa. But as the company left Saint Louis, she admitted a "peculiar" feeling pulling away from "the very border of civilization."[26] Where most women could vent their fears or displeasure with the journey west in letters, Narcissa felt bound by the restraints of her missionary role. She knew her letters would be shared among family, friends, and even published for strangers, so that "what I say to one I say to all."[27]

They traveled by horseback, usually sleeping in the open, riding hard for nearly a month to catch up with the Oregon-bound American Fur Company caravan of trappers and traders. The large group, "a moving village," Narcissa called it, of 70 men and hundreds of pack animals, offered safety. "Tell Mother," she wrote her siblings, "I am a very good housekeeper in the prairie."[28]

In early July, the party reached South Pass in the Rocky Mountains, marking an approximate halfway point for the journey. A few days later, they reached a rendezvous of hundreds of Indians, traders, and trappers along the Green River in present-day Wyoming. Narcissa marveled at the exotic blend of people—Flathead, Nez Percé, Snake, and Bannock tribes alongside rough-hewn mountain men. Narcissa and Eliza Spalding offered the Indians they encountered their first glimpses of white women. Narcissa wrote to Marcus's family, "I was met by a company of native women, one after the other, shaking hands and saluting me with a most hearty kiss. This was unexpected and affected me very much."[29]

But as they continued on toward Fort Hall on the Snake River (in present-day Idaho) with a group of traders and nearly 200 Indians, Narcissa formed new impressions of the native people. After watching the Native American women collecting wood, pitching shelters, cooking, and caring for the animals, she concluded the Indian women were "complete slaves of their husbands."[30] She was relieved when the Indians split off from the group.

By now, Narcissa was pregnant, and she turned to faith to sustain her and define her new role. She saw "the sustaining hand of God" in every good sign—good grazing for the oxen or a gift of food. But tensions and short tempers between the Whitmans and the Spaldings simmered the entire trip, affecting the journey.

They reached the Hudson's Bay Company trading post, Fort Walla Walla, in early September and then traveled down the Columbia River to the major trading post at Fort Vancouver. Narcissa found the Indians she met less and less impressive. The staring and attention no longer pleased her. She believed the Flatheads had no feelings for their children. As the cultural divide widened between Narcissa and the native people she met, she found the Indians lacking. The Whitmans had come to Oregon not to understand but to save the heathen's "perishing soul" from burning in hell.

Fort Vancouver on the Pacific Ocean sat in splendor as Great Britain's seat of power in Oregon. From here, tons of furs and trade goods from the North American West sailed for England. After 4,000 miles and six and a half months on the trail, Narcissa delighted in the sights, sounds, and especially, comforts of civilization. Narcissa and Eliza stayed here for several weeks while Marcus and Henry departed to look for suitable sites for their missions. Narcissa taught singing to the fort's young people and gathered supplies for her new home: tinware pails and coffee pots, bleached linen for sheets, and blankets. She even saved fruit seeds to plant in the spring.

The Spaldings would build their mission among the Nez Percé, and the Whitmans would settle among the Cayuse tribe at Waiilatpu, on a site about 25 miles east of Fort Walla Walla. Although Narcissa was encouraged to stay at Fort Vancouver through the winter, she insisted on setting out for her new home in November. She felt in high spirits—she was a missionary with a good husband and a baby on the way. "Our desire now is to be useful to these benighted Indians," she wrote missionary Samuel Parker, "teaching them the way of salvation . . . and the beauties of a 'well ordered life and godly conversation'; and to answer the expectations of those who sent us here. It is a great responsibility to be pioneers in so great a work. It is with cautious steps that we enter on it."[31]

The mission stood on the banks of the Walla Walla River with 300 acres for farming and building. A windowless small house, hastily constructed, had a heating stove in the living space, a large fireplace in the central kitchen, and two little bedrooms. With a few pieces of furniture, her items from Fort Vancouver, and even a dog and a cat, Narcissa felt satisfied with her new home. "These may appear small subjects to fill a letter with," she wrote, "but my object is to show you that people can live here, & as comfortably too as in many places east of the mountains."[32]

Nearby lay the winter lodges of a band of Cayuse, a people who spoke Nez Percé, which Narcissa had not yet mastered. In early January, she visited the village and noted the Indians seemed pleased that she had come. Like many missionaries, she felt ill at ease "in heathen lands . . . widely separated from kindred souls, alone, in the thick darkness of heathenism." This feeling challenged all missionaries in the field. The *Missionary Herald* had even warned that missionaries "must love the heathen in spite of their hatefulness." Narcissa, like any well-bred white woman, wished the assistance of servants to help run her little household. She quickly discovered Cayuse women would not do her work for her, and she lamented that they "do not love to work well enough for us to place any dependence upon them."[33]

The Whitmans began a worship service even as they struggled to establish a home and the mission itself. Homesickness overwhelmed Narcissa—even more so when she gave birth to a daughter, Alice Clarissa, in March 1837. The baby, the first child born to American citizens in the Pacific Northwest, became the center of Narcissa's life.

Narcissa and Marcus gradually established a schedule of worship and teaching. Both were hampered by the language barrier. Marcus gave sermons, and Narcissa taught hymns in English and later in the Nez Percé language. Narcissa started, and later abandoned due to ill health, a Bible class for women. The Whitmans often had a Sunday school, and Narcissa taught reading in her kitchen, though she struggled to communicate in the Cayuse tongue. Even a year later she admitted, "I cannot do much more than stammer yet in their language."[34]

Like other missionary wives, Narcissa didn't know how to go about her missionary work, struggled with doubts, and hoped, in a vague way, to have some sort of "gentle influence" on the Cayuse. But the culture seemed beyond her understanding. "We have had school," she wrote in 1838, "and my kitchen has been filled with children morn and eve, which has made my floor very dirty."[35] Narcissa, who had thrown her whole heart into the conversion of white sinners, using emotion and song and a deep desire to share the Word, found herself unable to reach out in the same way to the Cayuse.

For the Cayuse, the world—the earth, the animals, the plants—represented a sacred and holy place. For the Whitmans, God alone stood sacred. The Cayuse showed every sign of wanting to learn about Christianity, and some already knew how to pray with a partial knowledge of the Bible, taught by Hudson's Bay traders. They were willing to learn the secrets of white religion, just as they had benefitted from white trade goods and technology. Chants, songs, prayers, and rituals were already part of their spiritual life; adding elements of Christianity would not be difficult. They eagerly wanted to learn to read and write—a valuable tool and part of white people's power.

What the Cayuse came to realize was that missionaries like Narcissa and Marcus expected them to reject their own religious beliefs for the missionaries' views of faith. And many tribal customs like dancing, gambling, and horse racing would have to be rejected as well. The Whitmans also hoped to change the Cayuse life of seasonal hunting, fishing, and gathering to one of farming, the way people lived in "civilized" countries. For some Cayuse, the Whitman's constant harping on sin and evil seemed harsh. "Some feel almost to blame us for telling about eternal realities,"[36] wrote Narcissa. One Cayuse informed her that life was better when he didn't know that hunting, eating, drinking, and sleeping were bad.

With Marcus often away, sometimes for weeks, on mission business or treating the sick, Narcissa found life revolving more and more around little Alice. At age two, Alice recited Bible verses and talked of Jesus. Narcissa pledged to train Alice "for His glory." But Alice also imitated Cayuse ways and talked with the Indians. Like other missionary parents, this upset Narcissa. How was she to raise her daughter in a "heathen land, among savages?" Hawaiian missionaries warned Narcissa not to let Alice learn the native's language, and Narcissa came to believe she must devote more time to her daughter and less to the Cayuse.

The ABCFM decided to send several missionary families as reinforcements to Oregon to establish new missions. The families spent months with the Whitmans during the winter of 1838 and 1839. Tensions and sniping marked the relationships. No one was in charge; decisions about the missions were made and then reversed. Narcissa soon resented the extra people in her small home, especially when she felt the other wives did little to help her. She often retreated to her own room, seeming unfriendly and cold, where she struggled with these un-Christian impulses. Instead of forging a united front, the missionaries argued amongst themselves. They scattered to their separate missions and sent complaining reports back to the mission board. Eventually, in 1842 and 1843, Marcus traveled all the way to Boston to keep the ABCFM from shutting down some of the missions in Oregon. All this added strain to Narcissa's life.

In late June 1839, Narcissa's world fell apart. As Marcus and Narcissa sat reading, Alice announced she wanted a drink. The child wandered down to the river, where she fell in and drowned. As Narcissa grieved, she wondered if God was punishing her for loving Alice too much, for loving her daughter above him. As the weeks wore on and she struggled to cope, Narcissa decided that instead of punishment, "Jesus' love for her [Alice] was greater than mine."[37]

Narcissa continued to teach the Cayuse children, but she withdrew more from her missionary work. At the same time, Catholic missionaries competed for the Indians' attention, although according to staunch Presbyterians like Narcissa and Marcus, the Catholics would burn in hell right alongside the Indians. Why had she and Marcus failed to convert any of the Cayuse? Narcissa questioned her own abilities. "To be a missionary in name and to do so little or nothing for the benefit of heathen souls, is heart-sickening," she wrote a friend. "I sometimes almost wish to give my place to others who can do more for their good."[38] But then she blamed the Cayuse for ignoring their teachings, for being proud, vain, selfish, and ungrateful.

Over the years, the mission complex added new buildings, a larger house, a blacksmith shop, a gristmill, and a sawmill. The fields yielded bushels of fruits and vegetables, and a herd of cattle grazed in the pastures. About 50 Cayuse were farming, too. Narcissa's new home had a dining room and parlor and all manner of furniture. Pictures graced the walls, and the Whitmans dined on china. This was progress; this was civilization.

But this show of comfort and wealth irked many Cayuse, especially younger members of the tribe. Some felt that, because the Whitmans used and controlled the land, they should pay for it or leave. The farm's tilled fields gobbled up grazing land for Cayuse horses. To a culture that valued gifts as a show of friendship and hospitality, the Whitmans appeared stingy, offering goods only in exchange for work. But the Whitmans adamantly refused to pay for the land and turned a blind eye to Cayuse complaints, blaming a small faction of troublemakers.

Narcissa added new responsibilities to her household that turned her focus further from mission work. She took in two little girls, the half-Indian children of famed mountain men Joe Meek and Jim Bridger, and another "half-breed" boy. If she couldn't convert the Cayuse, she could at least shape and civilize these children. She kept the children away from the taint of the Cayuse, and she determined that they, unlike Alice, should speak nothing but English.

As the 1840s dawned, the Whitmans and the Cayuse faced a new transformation. It began with a trickle of Americans arriving in Oregon. Narcissa commented on the immigration in her letters home and concluded: "What a few years will bring forth we know not."[39] Once started, the flood carried more emigrants each year into Oregon and right to the Waiilatpu mission, which became a resting spot for weary travelers. Narcissa and Marcus both felt enthusiasm for Oregon's prospects.

When Marcus left for a year-long journey back to the states, Narcissa felt uneasy staying at Waiilatpu without him. One night, she was sure a Cayuse attempted to break down her bedroom door, intent on attacking her. She abandoned the mission after that and spent most of the next year socializing at Fort Walla Walla and Fort Vancouver and with a group of Methodist missionaries. To be in the company of "living and growing Christians is very refreshing to me, after having lived so much alone, immerged in care and toil," she wrote.[40] As soon as she departed the mission, the Cayuse burned down the gristmill. Narcissa saw no great meaning to the destruction and told herself that "the sensible part of the Cayuse feel the loss deeply."[41]

Marcus arrived back in the fall of 1843 with the largest group of emigrants yet, nearly 1,000 people. Narcissa reluctantly returned to Waiilatpu, plagued more often now by recurring health problems. But the following year, she took on another challenge: she agreed to raise the seven Sager children, orphaned by the death of both parents on the Oregon Trail. They ranged in age from 13 to five months old, five girls and two boys. One of the older girls noticed Narcissa's special hunger to care for the baby. The Sagers' arrival allowed Narcissa to completely withdraw from missionary work.

She blossomed during these years at the mission, with renewed health and energy. She set up schedules for the Sager children and supervised chores, schooling, and religious lessons, also doling out punishments when needed. She made more efforts to examine her own heart and curb her irritations. She felt hope for the future. The Whitmans even hired a schoolmaster each winter and invited other white children to come and learn.

If they could not easily convert the Cayuse, they could help convert ragged emigrants and give Oregon a new population of hardworking and God-fearing citizens. This proved familiar work for Narcissa; it was the work of conversion she'd known back home, work made easier by shared language, culture, and basic values. One young man wrote of her "large, soft" eyes and noted, "She seemed endowed with a peculiar magnetism when you were in her presence, so that you could not help thinking yourself in the presence of a much higher than the ordinary run of humanity. I have heard her pray, and she could offer up the finest petition to the Throne of Grace of any person I have ever heard in my life."[42]

Narcissa remained hopeful that the Cayuse would see the light. She believed the Indians truly liked the mission family. Spats of violence did not undo their regular pattern of coexistence, but there were noticeable changes. "The poor Indians," she wrote her mother, "are amazed at the overwhelming numbers of Americans coming into the country. They seem not to know what to make of it."[43]

Wrapped up in her adoptive and busy family, unwilling to admit failure with the mission, Narcissa again ignored warning signs all around her. When the United States and Great Britain agreed in 1846 to set a border granting a huge tract of land to the Americans, she believed the Cayuse would see how things were and settle down.

While some Cayuse still attended church services, in eleven years the Whitmans had failed to convert a single Indian to Christianity. The other missions had not done much better. The old dispute with the Cayuse over payment for the mission land had remained a simmering issue, and the influx of huge numbers of white pioneers raised the temperature to boiling. The Cayuse recognized that they faced displacement by the newcomers. Brief skirmishes occurred between whites and Indians. Emigrants' livestock ruined grazing lands and trampled the roots and camas bulbs the Cayuse depended on. The Whitmans gave charity to the white emigrants but charged the Cayuse for the use of the mill. White children went to school, while Indian children did not.

The worst blow fell in 1847 when a deadly measles epidemic, a disease brought by the emigrants, swept through the Cayuse village. By mid-November, nearly half the Cayuse had died; at the epidemic's height, four or five children died each day. And because Marcus Whitman was a doctor—but his healing potions did nothing to stop Indian deaths—the mission became a point of rage for many Cayuse. Some Cayuse even accused him of poisoning Indians.

Other whites recognized a dangerous situation brewing and warned Marcus. He worried, but he'd lived among the Cayuse for so long that he did not believe they would really hurt him. Narcissa, however, did fear they would all be killed. Elizabeth Sager recalled, "serious trouble was feared by them from the Indians. This talk was very guarded on their part, as they did not wish the fears of the children alarmed."[44]

On November 29, 1847, a band of Cayuse, their faces painted black and white, attacked the mission, killing Marcus and Narcissa and eleven other people. Marcus was cut down with a hatchet; Narcissa was shot, her face mutilated. Forty-seven people, mostly emigrants, survived the attack, but they were held prisoner for the next month until a trader from the Hudson's Bay Company negotiated their release.

The territory's new governor pursued the Cayuse for nearly two years until the Indians responsible for the Whitmans' deaths were turned over. Five Cayuse hanged for the crime, but this did not save the tribe. In 1848, Congress passed a bill creating the Oregon Territory. There was no room for the Cayuse and other Indian people.

The killings ended the ABCFM's missions in Oregon. Narcissa had done her best, but she'd failed to understand the people she'd meant to help or to recognize how they might have seen her. As one friend wrote after her death, "It was the common remark among them that Mrs. Whitman was 'very proud.'"[45] After their deaths, Americans regarded Narcissa and Marcus Whitman as martyrs who'd died for their faith in the far, dark reaches of "heathendom."

Miriam Davis Colt

An Experiment in Kansas

"What I crave must be gained by my own effort," wrote Miriam Davis, one of 17 children born to a poor family in New York City.[46] At age 15, she went to work, sewing and cleaning for hire. All the while she paid for her own schooling, and after eight years Miriam earned a teacher's certificate. She married a fellow teacher, William Colt, and began a family in Montreal, Canada.

Eleven years later, William announced he required "more of Heaven's pure air," and Miriam reluctantly agreed to pull up stakes and move with their children, Willie and Mema, to Kansas. She copied down the lyrics of a new song, the refrain sweeping people up in the excitement of the west: "Ho, brothers! Come brothers! Hasten all with me, We'll sing, upon the Kansas plains, The song of liberty."

The Colts purchased shares in an experimental vegetarian colony settling in Kansas. William's parents and sister, Lydia, also joined the venture. The Vegetarian Company, with a written constitution and elected directors, would make preparations, build a gristmill and sawmill, and have a boardinghouse ready for settlers to live in while they built their own new homes. Miriam believed that, by joining a ready-made community, her

Sheet music for a popular song promoting Kansas, 1856. *Library of Congress*

family might avoid the hardships experienced by so many pioneers. With the promise of a good climate, "where fruit is so quickly grown," and with people whose taste and habits would match their own, she felt the venture might pay off handsomely.

In April 1856, the Colt family began their journey west from New York via stagecoach and then train, finally reaching Kansas City on a steamer ship around the first of May. The word "city" seemed a stretch to Miriam, who observed that "it takes but a few buildings in this western world to make a city." Outfitted with wagons, oxen, and provisions, they began the next leg of their journey, leaving steam power behind, wrote Miriam, to "try the virtue . . . in ox-power."

Miriam resolved to make the best of things. After all, the whole point of the new community was the well-being of the members, achieved through abstaining from meats and alcohol, throwing themselves into work, and assembling frequently for uplifting discussions to secure "strength of body and vigor of mind."

They slept in the wagon or lodged in houses along the route, shelters that "would only pass for apologies for houses at the north," thought Miriam. At one farm, she couldn't help noticing the wife's downtrodden appearance, her feet bare and a white sack carrying a few quarts of cornmeal twisted up and thrown over her shoulder. Is this what I shall come to? Miriam wondered.

Kansas also faced tensions between "border ruffians," who desired the spread of slavery into the territory, and free-soil settlers, who opposed slavery, like the Colts. "These Bandits have been sent in here, and will commit all sorts of depredations on the Free State settlers," wrote Miriam, "and no doubt commit many a bloody murder."

But her pen also captured the spring beauty all around her, even as her wagon sat mired in a mudhole and the family lunched on soda biscuits. She inhaled deeply "the sweet odor that comes from the blossoms of the crab-apple trees that are blooming in sheets of whiteness along the roadside." Another day she wrote of "flowers blooming at our feet, and grasshoppers in profusion hopping in every direction."

On May 12, the party decamped with high hopes, expecting to arrive at their new home by nightfall. Miriam envisioned an escort to lead the new settlers into town and a rifle salute. Instead, a steady rain pelted down, and they discovered their new home was nothing but a large campfire surrounded by tents—no snug boardinghouse. Women sat inside a large center tent grinding corn in hand mills. The tent held a stove, and for supper they dined on corn cakes, stewed apples, and tea.

More discouraging news hit the family the next day—no sawmill or gristmill had been built, something their investment money was supposed to have helped pay for. And there was only a single plow for the whole community. The lack of proper building materials from the promised sawmill hampered any attempt to build a home of more than canvas, bark, and wooden shakes.

Miriam and William moved their family from the tent village to the actual settlement site a mile away. Here they found a log cabin, measuring 16 feet by 16 feet, where the future community center would be. With a few other families, they set up there, laying a stone floor, flooring the loft, and adding a few shelves to hold plates and utensils. They sat on trunks and lay wagon boards across a washtub for a table. A blanket covered the doorway, but even weighted down it failed to block the wind. The Colt family set up housekeeping in the loft of the log cabin, sleeping on the floor atop a mattress stuffed with prairie grass. They shared the loft space with another family. More people slept on the stone floor below, wrapped in blankets.

Just a week later, many of the company who'd traveled to Kansas with the Colts departed. In the midst of the disheartening news that many families had already left, the Colts tried to make the best of things, although, as Miriam described it, "a heavy weight is resting upon each one's heart." She wondered, "Can anyone imagine our disappointment?"

Miriam also reveled in the beauty all around her and wrote often of the flowers and trees, the sunsets, and the lovely glow of the moon in a starlit sky. But certain elements of their new home, like the nightly howls of the wolves, inspired fears that outweighed the beauty. Sometimes Indians dropped by the house, sitting on the chairs and frightening Miriam, Willie, and Mema with their "painted" faces. The nearly nude forms of the men made her "shudder." Rattlesnakes slithered in the grass and got in the house, and she feared letting Willie and Mema go outside.

The effort needed for everyday chores like washing and cooking caused constant headaches. Miriam did laundry in a creek, fuming that the company secretary, the man in charge, who was supposed to purchase necessary items, might have thought of soap! Clothes dried out in the sun, and Miriam feared Native Americans would steal their garments. She cooked outdoors, hampered by prairie winds that blew ashes, dirt, and smoke. "The bottom of our dresses are burnt full of holes now," she lamented, "and they will soon be burnt off." Before long, necessity drove her to don the Bloomer costume, a knee-length dress worn over ankle-length full trousers, which allowed some freedom of movement.

Summer invited illness and hordes of invading mosquitoes. Miriam nursed the sick, cooked and lugged water for those in need, and even picked little bouquets of flowers to cheer people suffering with chills and fever. Everything meant more work: a storm dissolved the mud chinking in the shared log house and spattered mud over everything, which meant that dishes, beds, blankets, and people had to be cleaned. Miriam wondered at the changes that cooking and living outdoors had brought: "Put a blanket over my head, and I would pass well for an Osage squaw," she commented. Her hands were the color of smoked ham, the skin peeling and burned.

The farm the Colts purchased lay about two miles from the community center, bordering lands of about 4,000 Osage Indians whose village lay across the Neosho River. Lands belonging to William's parents and his sister Lydia connected with their property. But with only one plow and every man wanting to get his seed in, William often plowed at night under moonlight. They planted corn and vegetables and made plans to build their cabin. William called the place an elegant building spot and promised a neat little log home. When the one plow broke, William's father took it to the nearest blacksmith 25 miles away for repairs.

When some of the company-promised supplies finally arrived, the Colts discovered they had to pay an exorbitant amount for goods they'd already paid money to help buy. The family's corn and other vegetables were shooting up through the rich soil, but for the time being, everyone lived on cornmeal cooked up as johnnycakes and corn pudding served with milk. Precious wheat bread was reserved for William's parents to eat.

Sickness stalked the family, and more trouble arrived when, by the first of July, the water dried up. William and Miriam discussed leaving, but William's father declared he would not go and neither would his wife or daughter. The old man yoked up the oxen and headed for his claim four miles out, seeking water. Miriam and her husband felt they could not abandon the rest of the family and went with them. The claim had an "old Indian house" in which they could live—but it was on Indian land.

Miriam worried the Osage would return from their summer hunting trip and find them there, "and I know not what our fate would be," she wrote.

At the house, they slept on the floor, and Miriam tended to each family member as they fell sick. Miriam, too, suffered with headaches, weakness, and dizzy spells. But she dragged herself from her mattress to do a few chores, sitting down when exhaustion and her pounding head crippled her. By mid-July Miriam's composure nearly shattered as she looked at her family and in-laws lying on the floor, tossing and turning with raging fevers and begging for water that Miriam was too weak to fetch. Finally, a neighbor lent them one of his hired hands to cut wood, bring water, and care for the livestock. "Just three months to-day," wrote Miriam, "since we left home; mark the contrast!"

Miriam and William suffered a bad blow to their fortunes when their oxen ran off and couldn't be found. Miriam spent several days looking for the precious work animals, even enlisting a neighbor's help. The man loaned her a horse, which she rode astride in her bloomers—an unladylike pose that was shocking to her—but her neighbor "made no remark, and like a gentleman, as he was, never seemed to notice my position." When she reached home and jumped off the horse, William smiled at her and asked, "Why, Miriam, what will you do next?"

With the return of the Osage—who frequently stole melons, pumpkins, and corn from the settlers' fields—Miriam felt too afraid to stay on Indian lands. They returned to the log cabin in the unfinished community. Now nearly penniless, Miriam and William determined to leave the community behind, driven out by sickness, the loss of their oxen, and fear of the Indians. They tried unsuccessfully to recoup some of their investment in the Vegetarian Company scheme. Sadly, William's parents and sister stubbornly remained behind, and several months later, Miriam heard that all three had died.

The Colts sold their wagon and whatever else they could, and they made arrangements to travel with others leaving for Saint Louis. One man in the party drank heavily and said he was a border ruffian, willing to kill them. Miriam did her best to calm him, but the family hastily left and joined a teamster and his son heading east. The water along the route was bad, covered in green scum, and though Miriam boiled it into tea, she hated for her children to have to drink such water "full of disease."

They stopped in a town for help when Willie fell gravely ill, but the townfolk seemed more appalled by Miriam's bloomers than the family's plight. She spent a dark week of daily nursing and sleepless nights, hoping Willie would take a turn for the better but fearing the worst. When Willie died on September 24, she gently closed her son's eyes and woke her husband, who was also sick. Only nine days later, William died too, and Miriam stepped "out on the sea of life alone," half her family ripped from her side in a few short days. She couldn't give up; she knew she must think of her daughter, Mema.

Stranded, Miriam sold what little she had left for gravestones and traveling money. Townspeople helped her redeem an insurance policy William had left and make arrangements to return to New York with Mema. Once there, she purchased a few acres of land, only to lose her farm to foreclosure a few years later. In an attempt to support herself and her daughter, Miriam wrote about their ill-fated colony in *Went to Kansas*, published in 1862. It detailed the few short months during the summer of 1856—the early days of Kansas settlement—when she faced disappointment, hardship, and heartbreaking loss.

Frances Grummond

Army Wife in Wyoming

Winding through the wilds of Wyoming on the way to Fort Phil Kearny in the fall of 1866, Frances Grummond earned her stripes as a new army wife the hard way. Wearing soft cloth slippers for comfort while jostling and jolting around in the back of an army ambulance wagon, Frances had climbed out to answer the call of nature. She forgot to tell the driver to wait, and when she returned to the trail, the wagon and her party had ridden off into the distance!

Grummond started to run after them, smashing through a patch of prickly cactus that punctured the slippers and sank cactus needles into her feet. She couldn't stop, though; the wagons plodded on a good distance away, and fear of Indians sent her scampering in acute pain for nearly a mile. She reached her party and collapsed, exhausted and speechless. She had to be lifted into the wagon, where she spent the next two days of her journey tearfully pulling cactus needles from her feet.

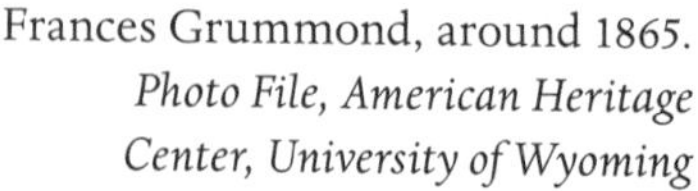

Frances Grummond, around 1865.
Photo File, American Heritage Center, University of Wyoming

Wyoming was a long way from her home in Franklin, Tennessee, where Frances had met her husband, George Grummond, a Union officer, during the Civil War. In August 1865, a few months after the war's end, they married. She'd quickly learned her first lesson about the life of an officer's wife: packing, unpacking, and constant upheaval marked the days. Grummond's orders, as an officer of the newly organized 18th US infantry, sent the young couple first to New York, then to Vicksburg, Mississippi, and finally west to the new fort in Wyoming Territory.

The government had opened a shortcut for gold seekers traveling to Montana, a road through the Powder River country that wound around the Big Horn Mountains. Known as the Bozeman Trail, the road cut through the heart of prime hunting lands of the Lakota Sioux. At Fort Laramie in June 1866, government negotiations with Chief Red Cloud and other Indian leaders to gain use of the lands were interrupted by the arrival of Colonel Henry Carrington, sent to build and command a line of new forts. Red Cloud stormed out of the meetings, incensed at the arrogance and manipulations of the government, which had sent soldiers, in his words, "to steal the road before the Indians say Yes or No." Red Cloud's warriors began a guerilla warfare campaign of resistance against the military invasion of their lands.

Meanwhile, Frances and George Grummond traveled west by train, steamboat, and army ambulance (a vehicle Frances came to despise over the 1,000 miles of travel). She yearned to escape the bumpy confines for freedom on horseback and grumbled at the army's lack of concern for the comfort of female travelers bound to follow their husbands. A few months pregnant, Frances only hinted through her writings of her "delicate condition."

The Grummond's journey into the "heart of a hostile Indian country," with only a mail party and an escort of six men, kept

Frances's nerves on edge the entire trip. Every beautiful mountain, hill, canyon, and ridge seemed alive with a "hidden foe." They stopped at ranches and forts along the way or slept in the wagons with straw pillows and gray wool army blankets for bedding. Buffalo chips and dried sage brush supplied fuel when wood proved nonexistent.

Food consisted mostly of canned goods and bread; however, this "greatly simplified the preparation of meals, fortunately for me, in the absence of knowledge in the culinary art,"[47] acknowledged Frances, who'd been raised in a Southern household with enslaved cooks. During a short stay at Fort Laramie, about 250 miles from their destination, the Grummonds ate at the officers' dinner table, or "mess," to spare Frances the ordeal of cooking.

Eighty miles from Fort Phil Kearny, they glimpsed towering Cloud Peak, their first view of the Bighorn Mountains. Frances's joy at finally arriving shattered as they halted outside the fort's gates to allow a wagon to pass. It carried "the scalped and naked body" of a member of the wood train, a detail of soldiers that sallied forth each day to cut timber for finishing the fort and building a stockpile of wood for the winter. She found consolation in the fact that the four other women living at the fort were officers' wives "who extended their kindly and sisterly greetings. Hope sprang up!" Frances discovered, however, that "not a stick of timber could be cut, nor a load of hay secured for the garrison without conflict." But she found this reality easier to bear in the reassuring and comforting presence of other women.

As the Grummonds' quarters were still unfinished, Frances set up housekeeping in two tents drawn together, the first for storage and the other holding two hospital bunks and a small heating stove. A few feet away, a tarpaulin covered a cook stove. That first night, snow drifted into the tents, covering Frances's face and her and her husband's bedding and clothes.

In the morning, after shaking snow from her shoes and stockings, she tackled breakfast. A soldier had brought wood and fired up the cook stove. Frances bravely fried bacon, boiled coffee, and whipped up a batch of rock-hard biscuits mixed from flour, salt, and water. But when she grabbed a butcher knife to chop the biscuits, she nearly severed her thumb instead.

Another morning, she started a brisk fire with some wood shavings, an abundant fuel due to the fact that the fort lay under construction. But the wind blew sparks from her fire under the commanding officer's quarters, setting ablaze accumulated carpentry debris. The fire was quickly extinguished, but the Grummonds were moved to a large hospital tent where Frances's cooking stove had more room. "My cooking experiments were never a great success," she confided. Further failures included pies that oozed out all the filling and a soup made with dried, compressed vegetables, which swelled and swelled in the simmering water, while Frances frantically ladled the growing mess out of the pot.

Throughout the fall, Frances felt the constant stress of alarms as Indians attacked the wood train, ran off horses and cattle, and cut off any person venturing too far from the stockade gates. Her world "revolved in a very small space," and she feared the Lakota would climb over the stockade wall under cover of darkness. Sometimes Indians galloped along the ridges in full view of the fort, waving blankets and taunting the soldiers with whooping war calls. She felt a bit safer when they traded the tents for their new quarters of pine logs and a real roof.

Fort life also brought comforts and cheer. The post's band and string section uplifted spirits with marital tunes, dance music, and hymns. With five ladies at the fort, "each had four places to visit," noted Frances, where they compared notes on life and played games of cards. The dedication of the fort's flagpole on October 31, a glorious blue-sky day, brought tears to Frances's eyes as the soldiers in full dress uniforms passed for review, and the huge flag rose above the fort accompanied by the golden notes of "The Star-Spangled Banner" and "Hail Columbia." That evening, Margaret Carrington, the commander's wife, hosted dancing, singing, and "general merrymaking" at headquarters.

Frances felt more secure when a long-awaited group of reinforcements—mostly raw recruits—reached Fort Phil Kearny. Her husband joined several of the newly arrived officers in expressing the opinion that a more aggressive stance was necessary toward the Lakota. The men, including George Grummond and newly arrived Captain William Fetterman, soon got their wish.

Flags signaling another attack on the wood train sent the fort into action on the morning of December 6. Frances's husband rode with the group sent to relieve the wood train. Two men were killed that day, and George Grummond barely escaped with his life. "A sense of apprehension," Frances wrote, "that I seemed to have been conscious of ever since my arrival at the Post, deepened from that hour. No sleep came to my weary eyes, except fitfully, for many nights, and even then in my dreams I could see him riding madly from me with the Indians in pursuit."

All remained quiet until the successful December 19 rescue of the wood train from attack. But hundreds of Indians had been sighted, and no one knew how many Lakota and their allies had amassed in the vicinity of Fort Phil Kearny. The fort had only 350 men, including soldiers, civilians, teamsters, and other employees. To make matters more desperate, ammunition had run low, with long-expected supplies never arriving.

Two days later, on December 21, the wood train departed, heavily armed and with a guard of 90 men. When the attack came, 81 men, including George Grummond, rode to the rescue. Colonel Carrington ordered Captain Fetterman, in charge of the relief, to support the wood train and report back, and under no conditions was he to chase the Lakota beyond Lodge Trail Ridge.

Standing in the doorway of their house, Frances was "filled with dread and horror at the thought that after my husband's hairbreadth escape scarcely three weeks before he could be so eager to fight the Indians again." A fellow officer, reminding Grummond of his wife's advancing pregnancy, urged him not to do anything rash.

Word soon came back that the wood train had made it safely to the pinery, but Fetterman had charged on with his men, including George Grummond, beyond the crest of Lodge Trail Ridge. Carrington ordered out the infantry to aid Fetterman. When volleys of rapid shots shattered the cold December air, everyone recognized the sounds of a desperate fight—and then, dead silence. "Less than half an hour had passed," recorded Frances, "and the silence was dreadful." Fetterman and the 81 men under his command had chased several hundred Lakota decoys over the ridge and into the midst of Red Cloud's warriors.

Frances gathered with the other women for the painful wait. By nightfall, wagons carrying the stripped and mutilated bodies of 49 men rolled into the fort, "with the heart-rending news . . . that probably not a man of Fetterman's command survived." Margaret Carrington took Frances into her arms and then into her home, "where in silence we awaited the unfolding of this deadly sorrow." Everyone feared that at any moment the weakened fort would come under attack.

Colonel Carrington promised Frances he'd retrieve her husband's body from the field of battle. Before the rescue detail left, Carrington ordered that, in case of an attack, the women and children must go into the powder magazine with supplies of food. But, in a last desperate struggle, they should be blown up with the ammunition and guns rather than be captured alive.

During those long hours of waiting, Frances sat at her window. Finally, more wagons rumbled into the fort, and Carrington entered the room and handed her an envelope containing a lock of George Grummond's hair. Her husband had also worn a miniature painting of Frances, and she wondered which Lakota warrior wore this as a trophy of victory. Christmas arrived to the sad sound of hammers and saws preparing coffins. Frozen men dug 10-foot deep trenches in the snow so the Indians could not scale the stockade walls.

January 1867 brought fresh orders when a command of new soldiers finally arrived at Fort Phil Kearny. The Carringtons would transfer to new command headquarters, and Frances, who planned to return home with her husband's body, prepared to leave, too. Frances outfitted herself for below-freezing temperatures with buffalo-fur boots, fur robes, shawls, and cloaks. Carpenters fit the wagons with small stoves and smoke holes, while bins of pine blocks and knots were readied for the journey. Frances also took a mattress and a chair, and the remaining women at the fort purchased her minimal furniture and dishes, "paying double their value" so she might have money for the journey. The wagons, with an escort of 60 men, rolled out of the fort on January 23 and floundered through the deep snow, covering only six miles in eight hours.

Bitter cold turned the journey into a march of misery. At one point, Margaret Carrington's thermometer gave up, the mercury congealed in the bulb. Carrington ordered the soldiers' legs whipped to keep the circulation moving, but many later lost ears, fingers, feet, and limbs to frostbite. Cooking proved nearly impossible, hatchets broke off chunks of frozen food, and the snow melting around the campfire quickly froze into rings of ice. The mules seemed driven crazy by the cold—breaking loose, kicking, biting, and, in their hunger, trying to eat wagon spokes and canvas covers. At one point, the command had to descend a 60-foot river embankment. "When my turn came," wrote Frances, "I rolled over on my bed, clung for dear life to the sides of the wagon, with eyes shut and jaws clamped . . . for it all depended upon those mules." Fortunately, a few Indian scares turned out to be nothing.

Frances found her brother William waiting for her at Fort Laramie; her family had received a telegram telling of the Fetterman disaster, and he'd left right away to reach Frances. Here she parted company with the Carringtons. The journey continued with a dangerous crossing of the iced-over Platte River. Finally, near Fort McPherson, Nebraska, they reached the Union Pacific Railroad and could continue the journey by train and then boat. After seven weeks, Frances Grummond reached her Tennessee home in March 1867. A month later, she gave birth to a baby boy.

Two strange twists of fate awaited Frances. She discovered that George Grummond had been married at the time he married her. George was not yet divorced from his first wife, the mother of his two children. Then, in 1870, Frances learned that Margaret Carrington had died, and she penned a note of sympathy to Henry Carrington. "Correspondence ensued that resulted in our marriage in 1871," she wrote in her memoirs. Their marriage lasted 40 years, and the couple had three children.

In 1908, Frances and Henry traveled to the site of Fort Phil Kearny, long since burned by Red Cloud's warriors. They went for the dedication of a monument marking "Massacre Hill," the spot where gentle Frances Grummond had lost her husband on that icy December day in 1866.

3

A WOMAN THAT CAN WORK

"Was I ever thrilled, seventeen years old and earning so much! I earned it all right."

—Montana schoolteacher, 1886

Women who rolled up their sleeves and provided lonesome miners or cowboys with tasty home cooking, clean clothes, sewing, and friendly company could earn a purse full of cash. Fifteen to twenty dollars a week could be had for scrubbing clothes. Luzena Wilson, newly arrived in Sacramento, earned five dollars for cooking a single breakfast and could have asked twice the price and been paid. Farmwomen turned rare but longed-for items like eggs, butter, and fresh-grown vegetables or sewn goods such as shirts, vests, and gloves into money. During the early days in a new Western home, women often supported their families while husbands tackled mining or began farming.

Primitive conditions, however, made this backbreaking work all the harder. Mollie Sandford traveled to a California silver mine with her husband and agreed to cook for the men. "My heart sinks within me," she wrote, "when I see eighteen or twenty [men], and no conveniences at all."[1] Another woman in 1851 listed her chores at a boardinghouse: washing, ironing, baking, cooking, setting and clearing a 30-foot-long table, feeding chickens, making soap and candles, and sewing sheets. She also babysat and nursed the sick. "But I would not advise any Lady to come out here and suffer the toil and fatigue that I have suffered for the sake of a little gold," she wrote a friend back home.[2] Another California woman, proud of her hard labor, claimed, "Had I not the constitution of six horses I should have been dead long ago."[3]

Fallen Women

Women with names like Irish Queen, Peg-Leg Annie, Squirrel Tooth Alice, and Contrary Mary earned livings as prostitutes, working mining, cattle, and railroad towns and military forts. White, African American, Mexican, Native American, and Asian women, mostly young and impoverished, worked this shady and dangerous life on the fringes of society.

Between 1865 and 1886, prostitution was the largest source of paid employment for women in Helena, Montana, with similar situations in many other towns. For some women, poor and uneducated and often used to lives of abuse, prostitution was the only way to survive.

Most prostitutes made little money, seldom earning enough to leave the profession. With payments to madams, room rent, and court fines, the women had little cash and few possessions. Prostitutes worked in dance halls and saloons; brothel workers claimed the most status, while the lowliest prostitutes walked the streets seeking clients.

Thousands of immigrant Chinese women were sold by their poor families into prostitution and virtual slavery in the West. The problem was especially bad in San Francisco, a mining boomtown, and in areas of the Rocky Mountain West. A number of Chinese and American women tried to end the practice by rescuing young women from their "owners."

At military posts near Indian reservations, some Native American women traded sexual favors for goods. A Montana Indian agent wrote, "The Indian maiden's favor had a money value, and what wonder is it that, half clad and half starved, they bartered their honor . . . for something to cover their limbs and for food for themselves and their kin."[4] Sexually transmitted diseases spread among the Indian populations. Other women at military forts, working as laundresses or in the sutler's store

Squirrel Tooth Alice, a "fallen woman" who worked in Kansas and Texas. *www.legendsofAmerica.com*

as "servants," were also prostitutes. The military mostly turned a blind eye to what went on inside the forts or in towns just outside.

Crime and prostitution blended in a vortex of violence. Belle Warden, an African American madam in Denver, and her employee Mattie Lemmon went to prison for slitting a customer's throat. In Idaho, Fannie Clark participated in a murder committed by three customers. Seventeen-year-old Maggie Moss of Denver took part in an armed robbery. Prostitutes stole from one another and from clients. They verbally abused each other and fought. "One-Arm" Annie Ferguson stole Emma Halbring's scarf and towels. The incident forced Ferguson to leave Laramie, Wyoming, for Cheyenne, where another prostitute, Fanny Brown, beat Ferguson to death. The 19th century treasured its notions of ideal womanhood, where virtuous women protected society's moral values. Prostitutes broke the rules, so it was believed the women deserved what they got and the lives they led.

Some prostitutes married, their choice of mates coming from the dregs of society whom they encountered in their jobs. The men lived by crime and often lived off their wives. A prostitute's marriage sometimes ended in her murder by her husband. Children of prostitutes led lives of poverty and uncertainty, and teenage daughters often followed their mothers into the profession.

Prostitutes faced dangers from themselves as well as clients, husbands, and other prostitutes. Women suffered from alcoholism and drug use and were frequently arrested for drunk and disorderly conduct. Many died from overdoses of morphine, laudanum, chloroform, opium, and even strychnine. The most common means of leaving prostitution was suicide, a sad comment on the lives of women who worked this unforgiving trade on the American frontier.

A Paying Job

Of course more respectable forms of paid employment also existed for women. Jobs outside the home reflected what 19th-century society considered proper for a woman. Nurturing occupations, such as teaching and domestic work, earned the most approval. The sphere of suitable jobs ranged from seamstress and milliner to servant, cook, waitress, and nurse. As childbirth neared, many women trusted the services of a midwife, a fellow female, over a male doctor.

Unmarried women, many still teenagers, made up the majority of teachers in the West. Teaching offered a paying job outside a woman's typical role of housework. Paid little, teachers often boarded with the families of their students. These young women taught in one-room schoolhouses built from sod or logs,

A young teacher surrounded by her students, Oklahoma Territory.
National Archives

or in no school at all, just a meeting space outdoors. Equipped with few supplies, teachers relied on whatever books and slates children brought from home. In some cases, the teacher possessed little more education than her students. Pupils ranged in age from five to 18 years, and sometimes older boys weren't about to behave for a female teacher younger than themselves.

One Kansas teacher's new schoolhouse had a cellar, but no door had yet been built to reach it. When a tornado twisted to earth and headed for her school, the teacher grabbed a firewood hatchet and chopped through the floor so her students could crawl down into the cellar. Luckily, the tornado veered off in another direction. Folks teased the schoolmarm about scaring the tornado away with her hatchet. Discipline, they said, should come easy to her after that.

Catholic and Protestant female missionaries headed west to convert Native Americans to Christianity, white culture, and white values. The earliest missionaries, however committed to their calling, faced enough of a struggle just to survive. One Oregon woman wrote, "I sometimes feel discouraged and fear I shall never do anything to benefit the heathen and might as well have stayed at home. . . . Last week I went four times to teach the Indians. But it is all I can do to get along, do my work, and take care of my children."[5] Many missionaries feared Native Americans had little interest in embracing the Bible, and living in the midst of an alien "savage" culture proved too much for most 19th-century white Americans. In the case of Narcissa Whitman, missionary life ended in tragedy and death.

Many Western women earned their living at less traditional jobs. Helen MacKnight Doyle and Bethenia Owens-Adair became doctors. Wives took charge of all sorts of family businesses after the deaths of their husbands. Some women worked as reporters, typesetters, printers, artists, telegraphers,

Newspaperwomen setting type in Kansas, 1880s. Notice the ruffled, feminine lampshade. *Kansas State Historical Society*

photographers, and even miners. Gender roles blurred more in the West than back east. And in towns with only a handful of adult citizens, everyone was needed—male and female—to keep the post office, newspaper, and general store running.

While many African American women in the West worked as maids or cooks, several earned reputations in business. Bridget "Biddy" Mason, a slave, and her three daughters trudged from Mississippi to Utah in 1847 with her master, Robert Smith, a member of the Church of Jesus Christ of Latter-Day Saints (or Mormonism). In 1851, Smith moved his family and slaves to a new Mormon settlement in Southern California. California had entered the nation as a free state, and when Smith prepared to move again in 1854, this time to slave-holding Texas, Biddy secured the help of a Los Angeles sheriff to remain in California.

Through the courts she won her right to freedom—and the freedom of her daughters and several other black women and children—in 1856.

Mason saved money working as a nurse and midwife, and within 10 years she bought her first plots of land in downtown Los Angeles, making her one of the first African American women in the United States to buy property. Over the years, Mason purchased and sold real estate and built commercial buildings on her lots, renting out space and earning a large fortune. She turned her blessings into generosity by donating land and money for churches, grocery stores, and schools. In 1872, she helped found the Los Angeles branch of the First African Methodist Episcopal Church, the city's first black church. When she died in January 1891, Biddy Mason left behind a fortune in real estate and the goodwill of her city.

Another African American woman, Sallie Fingers, owned a popular restaurant in Dodge City, Kansas. In this rough-and-tumble cattle town, Fingers dared to forbid swearing, drinking, and fighting in her establishment. The Dodge City census recorded Fingers' business as the only one in town owned by a woman.[6]

Working on the Land

The majority of Western women made their living from the land, on their own or alongside their husbands. On a ranch, a woman usually ran the dairy side of the business. But sometimes women performed other ranch chores, from herding, branding, and running cattle drives to keeping the account books. "I have tried every kind of work this ranch affords and I can do any of it," wrote a female rancher. "I just love to experiment, to prove out things, so ranch life and 'roughing it' just suits me."[7]

Farmwomen lent a hand with plowing and planting and tended the farm animals. Homesteading families on the plains faced tremendous hardships in earning a living from the land. The sod's tangle of thick, long roots snapped plow blades. Wind and heat withered crops. From June 1859 until November 1860, Kansas and Nebraska suffered a devastating drought that dried soil to dust.

As the prairie grass browned under the blazing sun each summer, people lived in dread of fire. Huge walls of flame and smoke would blacken the prairie sky, surging over the plains, fanned by the winds. Besides plowing a trench and lighting backfires to meet the blaze, farmers had little chance to fight back and often lost everything.

Millions of grasshoppers destroyed the hopes of plains farmers in the 1870s. The mighty swarms blocked the sun as they fell from the sky, thudding onto the ground like hail. A writhing mass four inches deep covered everything, while deeper drifts of the insects had to be shoveled from doorways. Families watched helplessly as grasshoppers devoured crops down to the ground, ate stored grain, and stripped trees of every leaf and twig. Worst of all, the unstoppable insects attacked settlers' homes, clinging to people's clothes and crawling inside where they gobbled curtains, bedding, furniture, and food in the cupboards. No means could fight the scourge, and the eggs the insects laid hatched the following summer to continue the devastation. No wonder many families gave up and retreated east.

"Have Not Spent an Idle Minute"

The main responsibility of every woman lay in the never-ending cycle of caring for her family. This vital role, carried out with few labor-saving devices, safeguarded her family's survival.

Chores on a given day included an exhausting round of milking cows and feeding chickens, caring for children, collecting fuel and water, washing dishes, cooking, baking, churning, mending, and housecleaning. "There was always something early and late," noted a pioneer woman from Texas.[8] "When I find so much that needs to be done, I can spare very little time to sleep," wrote another.[9]

Preparing food and preserving more for winter proved a constant labor. Especially in the early days of settlement, women turned raw resources into meals without the help of store-bought provisions. They milled grain for bread, milked

Laundry day in North Dakota, complete with copper boiler, washtub, and scrubboard. *Fred Hultstrand History in Pictures Collection, NDIRS-NDSU-Fargo*

cows, skimmed cream, churned butter, and made cheese. They grew vegetables and gathered wild fruit, ground raw meat, and stuffed their own sausages.

As with food, women often created clothing from scratch, too. Sheep yielded wool to be carded, spun, woven, sewn, or knitted. The most hated, backbreaking chore included buckets and a washtub, scrubboard, and battling stick. On laundry day, women simmered batches of lye soap, hauled and boiled water in huge tubs several times over, scrubbed, rinsed, and ironed. Flatirons for pressing clothes—made of a wedge of solid iron—heated on the stove or fire. One woman's recipe for laundry day included this 11-step routine that's exhausting even to read:

> 1. bild fire in back yard to het kettle of rain water.
> 2. set tubs so smoke won't blow in eyes if wind is peart.
> 3. shave 1 hole cake lie sope in bilin water.
> 4. sort things. make 3 piles. 1 pile white, 1 pile cullord, 1 pile work briches and rags.
> 5. stur flour in cold water to smooth then thin down with bilin water [for starch].
> 6. rub dirty spots on board. scrub hard. then bile. rub cullord but don't bile just rench [rinse] and starch.
> 7. take white things out of kettle with broom stick handle then rench, blew [whitener] and starch.
> 8. pore rench water in flower bed.
> 9. scrub porch with hot sopy water
> 10. turn tubs upside down
> 11. go put on a cleen dress, smooth hair with side combs, brew cup of tee, set and rest and rock a spell and count blessings.[10]

No wonder one woman claimed laundry day left her feeling like a "stewed witch!" And, as usual, even on laundry day, meals still needed to be cooked, children cared for, animals tended to, and so much more.

Women also worked at seasonal chores like drying fruit and vegetables and boiling batches of jams, candles, and soaps. They stuffed sausages and dried and smoked meats. Women helped bring in the crop and cooked huge meals for extra hands hired at harvest time. They sheared sheep in spring and prepared cloth during long winter nights. Women devoted weekly hours to sewing, mending, and darning worn clothes, their fingers flying as they plied needles and thread. They pitched in to build houses, dig wells and cellars, and defend their homes against Indians and outlaws. They worked in the fields, hunted and fished, and drove teams of horses into town.

A woman's work included doctoring her family through injury and illness—treating everything from broken bones to fever and snakebite—armed with common sense, homebrewed medicines, and prayer. Like other aspects of Western life, doctoring required ingenuity. A Kansas woman stitched a partially scalped man with fiddle string and her sewing needle. Another time, she removed a bullet with a knitting needle and a pair of pincers.

Child care in the West presented its own set of worries. Poor sanitation, limited knowledge of how disease spread, and no antibiotics allowed illness to claim young lives in horrifying numbers. The West also delivered a high rate of accidents when rattlesnakes, stinging insects, and wild animals lurked where children played. The plains' vastness could swallow up a wandering child. In mining towns, children tumbled down mine shafts and were run over in crowded streets. Mothers also feared the corruption of their young ones, exposed to unsavory saloons and gambling halls. An Idaho woman worried, "This is the hardest place to live upon principle I ever saw, and the young are almost sure to be led away."[11]

Few families escaped the loss of a child. A popular song of the time recalled listening for the little footsteps of a child now buried. One of a mother's most treasured possessions might be a photograph of her dead child, lying sleeplike on a bed. A whole family, grieving in their clothes of mourning black, might gather for a photograph around a deceased child displayed in his or her coffin. Perhaps they had no picture of their child taken in life.

Isolation from a midwife or even a neighbor woman caused some Western women to dread childbirth and made the recovery after giving birth more difficult. Frequently, mother or child—or sometimes both—died during the delivery. Martha Summerhayes, a young army wife in Arizona, felt especially isolated from the comfort of other women. "I knew nothing," she wrote, "of the care of a young infant, and depended entirely upon the advice of a Post surgeon . . . much better versed in the sawing off of soldier's legs than in the treatment of young mothers and babies."[12]

Overall, frontier women stretched, conserved, and made do to help their families survive. In the book *The Long Winter*, Laura Ingalls Wilder describes how her mother made a lamp from a button, a rag, and a small plate of grease. Women managed to cook custard without eggs or milk, bake apple pie without apples, brew coffee without coffee beans. Almost everyone knew what hunger was.

In the face of difficult conditions, frontier women worked hard, at home and at paying jobs, to insure the very survival of their families. No wonder then that, when the time came, everyone was ready for some fun and diversion.

Luzena Stanley Wilson

California Gold Fever

After four months on the road, Luzena Wilson, her husband, Mason, and their two small boys, Jay and Thomas, pulled into Sacramento, California, on the evening of September 30, 1849. Sacramento hummed with the activity of several thousand people, nearly all male. Traffic jams of mules and horses blocked muddy roads to and from the mines and river gullies. Hundreds of tents served as makeshift homes, while even more campfires illuminated where men slept on the ground, rolled up in blankets like so many cocoons.

Shopkeepers bartered and sold behind counters of boards slapped across barrels—each armed with scales to weigh the gold dust men used for currency. Coins were rare; people accepted a pinch of gold dust as a dollar, and everything cost *at least* one dollar. Luzena purchased a few supplies, including molasses and a slice of salt pork, for the dear price of one dollar each. The pork fizzled down to nothing, old and rotten after traveling around the tip of South America to the California coast. Her flour crawled with black worms, a disheartening sight at the end of the trail.

Luzena quickly learned she could make more money *off* the gold hopefuls than by mining alongside them. One morning, a man stopped at her outdoor fire. "Madame," he said to Luzena, "I want a good substantial breakfast, cooked by a woman." For five dollars, what seemed a princely sum, she fried two onions, two eggs, and a beefsteak, and boiled a cup of coffee. Afterward she reckoned, "If I had asked ten dollars he would have paid it."[13]

Businesses in the raw mining towns appeared and vanished in a flash. The Wilsons acted quickly. They sold their oxen within a few days and invested in a "hotel," one of the few wooden buildings in town. The place boasted a long living room, the walls stacked floor to ceiling with bunk beds. Here, men lay sick or sleeping, and one man lay dead, forgotten and overlooked. For her own brood, Luzena set up housekeeping in a tent with a dirt floor.

Women were so scarce—Luzena saw only two other women during six months in Sacramento—that men crowded her table, starved for homemade, female cooking. "It was hard work," she wrote, "from daylight till dark . . . hurried all day, and tired out," but her efforts paid off. After a few months, the Wilsons sold their interest in the hotel for $1,000 in golden dust.

Mason Wilson invested the money in barley, a commodity earning great profits, but misfortune began dogging the family when heavy rains caused the river to flood. Luzena was standing over her fire cooking when she first noticed rivulets trickling across the ground. Then a rush of water swooshed over her feet. She threw Tom and Jay onto the bed and grabbed all the things she could to keep them off the floor.

As the water rose, Luzena carried her boys to the hotel they'd just sold, a structure built three or four feet above the ground. She dumped them inside and hurried to gather more of the family's possessions, including their bedding and the dinner she'd just cooked. She struggled back to the hotel against swirling, knee-deep waters, the force nearly knocking her off her feet.

Within the hour, the whole town was afloat. By midnight, rising water forced the 40 people sheltering in the hotel to the upper floor. There they lived for the next 17 days, in the midst of rain, wind, and water, eating onions and anything they could snag floating by the windows. "Those were days of terror and fear," Luzena later recalled. They expected the quaking building to tumble into the torrent at any moment.

Sacramento, the Wilson's city of hope, lay in shambles. Sludge, debris, mold, and dead animals covered the town in a shroud of filth. "Our little fortune of barley gone," she wrote, "and I felt that I should never again be safe." The Wilson's tent had vanished, but their stove remained; they set up in the mud, walking over planks to reach the bed. Luzena awoke often during the night and reached down to feel if the water had risen.

With news of a new gold strike at Nevada City, the family decided to try their luck in another place. Without wagon, oxen, or money, they struck a bargain with a teamster to take Luzena, the children, and their few supplies to Nevada City for $700—Luzena herself was security for the "loan." She promised the man that if she lived, he'd get his pay. The trip of 60 miles took 12 days for there was no road, and the land had soaked up the winter rains and melting snows like a sponge. The little group spent hours digging the mules and wagon out of the mud. The miserable journey ended with a steep descent down a slippery rock face; the oxen locked their forelegs, and the animals and wagon slid a quarter mile down the mountain.

The ravines around Nevada City crawled with men armed with pickaxes and shovels or bent over in the knee-deep icy streams, washing soil from panned bits of gold. The Wilsons arrived covered in mud and too poor to afford a tent. Luzena and Mason cut pine branches and built a shelter. She set up the bedding and placed her stove under a pine tree. "I was established," she recorded, "without further preparation, in my new home."

When Mason left to split wood for a better structure, Luzena set about recouping the family finances. Down the road, she spied a tent with a sign that called the place a hotel, and Luzena determined to set up a rival establishment. With a few boards and a few stakes, she set up a table, bought provisions, and set to cooking. By the time Mason returned, 20 miners had chowed down at Luzena's makeshift table, each sprinkling a one-dollar pinch of gold dust in her hand as they left.

It seemed everybody around her had money, and the gold dust flowed like water from pockets. Rare fresh fruits and vegetables, even of miserable quality, sold as luxury items. A peach went for $2, and a watermelon might fetch $16! Again, miners willingly paid for home-cooked fare, and Luzena's efforts prospered once more. After six weeks, she paid back the $700 debt for her transportation from Sacramento.

Luzena's business expanded. She'd taken Mason "into partnership," and as the money rolled in, he'd built a house around the brush home and stove. They gradually added on rooms and took in renters who paid $25 a week. "I became luxurious," recalled Luzena, "and hired a cook and waiters. Maintaining only my position as managing housekeeper, I retired from active business in the kitchen."

The population of Nevada City, also called Coyote Diggins, exploded almost overnight. Luzena's hard work and never-say-die attitude amassed her family nearly $20,000 invested in the hotel and a small store. With no banks in town, men trusted her with their bags of gold dust, which she stored in milk pans, sometimes going to bed with more than $200,000 beneath her bed. She also kept a bag for storing money she made doing odd sewing jobs for the miners—a sideline that earned her hundreds of dollars in just a few months.

Luzena's business success paled, however, next to the professional gamblers who preyed on the restless miners always eager to risk their coins or bags of golden dust on a single bet. Thousands of men unleashed in a town filled with saloons and gambling tables—"they were possessed of the demon of recklessness," recalled Luzena—meant pistols and knives settled disputes and, one night, brought the danger to Luzena's front door.

With Mason away attending court, Luzena sat in her kitchen alone. Suddenly, fists pounded against the walls all around her house and contorted faces pressed against the windows. Cries of "Burn the house!" rent the darkness. Terrified and confused, Luzena opened the door and peaked out at the mob gathered around her hotel. Men shouted, "Search for him!" and "Burn him out!" The sheriff tried to explain that one of her boarders had murdered a gambler in the midst of a card game. Luzena had no choice but to let the mob search her place. The murderer remained undiscovered, and Luzena later learned he'd hidden in plain sight, disguised and standing not 10 feet away from her as part of the mob, watching her terror.

The good days in Nevada City ended abruptly for Luzena after 18 months. Instead of flood, this time fire consumed the town and the Wilsons' security. Warning cries and clanging bells in the night awoke the family, who escaped with nothing but their nightclothes. With everyone else, they stood helplessly while the town burned—the pine buildings were perfect tinder—turning the skies and surrounding forest into a blazing inferno. The imprint of that night, the buildings burning and crashing to the ground, the fire moaning "like a giant in an agony of pain," the smoldering ashes, the stricken faces of the homeless, the realization that her family had lost everything again, overwhelmed Luzena. For the first time her strength failed, "and I fell sick."

The Wilsons turned their backs on Nevada City and returned to the valley near Sacramento once again. They arrived to find a bloody dispute brewing—a squatters war. John Sutter had claimed much of the valley under Spanish land grants, and then

Sutter or his agents had sold off parcels under his grant titles. But the flood of newcomers to California ignored Sutter's grants and often squatted on the lands. The disputes between rival land claimants often turned bloody.

While the Wilsons pondered their next step, they took over an abandoned hotel, a place infested with hundreds of rats. The rodents scurried over the floors and raced from room to room through holes gnawed into the wood. The brazen creatures snapped at Luzena's heels and chewed the legs of the chairs as the family sat in them. At night, Luzena lay their bedding atop tables but couldn't sleep for fear of attacking rodents.

Sacramento had risen from the flood—a host of new brick buildings replaced ramshackle wooden dwellings and tents. Sidewalks protected against mud; actual stores, not just boards plopped across barrels, carried all manner of dry goods, food, and hardware. Civilized Sacramento had a bank, a photographer's shop, and mail delivery by pony express while stagecoaches and steamer ships constantly spewed forth new people. Luzena even attended the theater for a production of *Julius Caesar* at which a singer entertained the crowd during intermissions.

But the undercurrents of gambling, drunkenness, and violence remained, and only a month after the fire, Luzena and her family moved on from Sacramento. They traveled into the foothills, past wild oats and antelopes and elk. After several days, they set up camp near a stream under a canopy of an old oak tree. They slept in a tent made from tree boughs and the canvas covering from their wagon. The area belonged to a Spaniard, a rancher named Manuel Vaca.

Almost penniless again, Mason began cutting the oats and making hay to sell in San Francisco. Luzena once more dug in and began a hotel business, setting up her stove and camp kettle beneath a tree and making a sign that read WILSON'S HOTEL. She crafted a table from the wagon boards and used stumps and logs for chairs. Guests slept rolled up in bedding beneath a haystack, and for one dollar Luzena provided breakfast.

Once more her hotel prospered, and when the grass got stomped down to dust, she merely moved her stove. A row of nails hammered into tree trunks held her utensils, cups, and a shelf for plates. Her hotel earned a reputation as the best stop between Sacramento and Benicia.

Living amidst Spanish cowboys, Luzena thought nothing of traveling 12 miles on horseback to visit her nearest English-speaking female neighbor. The Wilsons also attended dances and feasts with their Spanish neighbors. The brilliant colors worn by the Spanish ladies amazed Luzena, who delighted in savory stews, piles of tortillas, hot chilies, and "tolerable whisky."

As fall approached, just as the family began building a house, rains and swollen rivers destroyed the hay crop they'd planned to use as partial payment for their land. The only answer was harder work at the hotel and attempts at farming for the next year. Then another blow fell, when a meeting of land commissioners in San Francisco declared that, "among the disputed boundary lines were those of the grant upon which we had bought," Luzena reported. Suddenly, surveyors and squatters staked out pieces of the Wilsons' land, even throwing up a crude cabin to mark their claims. Mason chased the squatters off with a rifle while Luzena waited, terrified he'd be killed by the squatters. It took years before the title of land was established in their favor; meanwhile, the Wilsons fought a continual battle with squatters.

As the years passed, Luzena gave birth to a daughter and helped establish a school for area children. With no local doctor, she also served as both physician and apothecary for neighbors, using a medicine chest left her by a physician who'd passed through. She dosed patients with calomel and quinine, felt pulses, and checked tongues. "I grew so familiar with the business that I almost fancied myself a genuine doctor," she noted, adding, "I don't think I ever killed anybody, and I am quite sure I cured a good many of my patients."

Like other Western women, Luzena Wilson, forty-niner, worked incredibly hard and persevered to keep her family financially secure, starting over with nothing more at hand than her own hard work and gumption. She rose from flood and fire to begin again, her story yet another tale of the fortunes won and lost in the early gold rush days of California.

Clara Brown

African American Pioneer

In early Colorado, pioneer Clara Brown's hard work, patience, and generosity turned the former slave into a beloved figure.

Clara, born around 1800 in Virginia, was taken by her master, Ambrose Smith, into Kentucky, at that time part of America's frontier. On Smith's farm, teenage Clara "married" a fellow slave named Richard and over the next few years gave birth to four children. One daughter drowned, and tragedy marked the family again when Smith died in 1835. In a cruel blow that shattered so many enslaved families, Clara's entire family was sold at auction to settle Smith's estate. On one horrendous day, she lost her husband; her son, Richard; and her daughters, Margaret and Eliza Jane. Clara herself was purchased by George Brown.

For the next 20 years, Clara served the Brown family, all the time seeking information about what had happened to her husband and children. She learned that her daughter, Margaret, had died. Her husband vanished from the records; her son was sold so many times that his trail ended too. Clara's life quest became finding Eliza Jane, a nearly impossible task.

George Brown's children granted Clara her freedom upon his death in 1857. Per Kentucky law, she had to leave the state within a year. Even with manumission papers, a former slave's freedom was never guaranteed—if caught in a slave state Clara could have been sold back into slavery.

At age 57, having known nothing of life but slavery, Clara headed to Missouri where she worked as a maid for a family that eventually moved west to Leavenworth, Kansas. Clara went with them, nurturing the slim hope that, with so many people heading west, Eliza Jane or someone who knew of her would be among them. Clara remained in Leavenworth for a year, staying behind and starting a laundry business when the family she worked for ventured on to California.

But news of gold strikes in Colorado pushed Clara into a decision of her own. At age 59, elderly by the day's standard, she would test her dreams against the wild and golden times in Colorado.

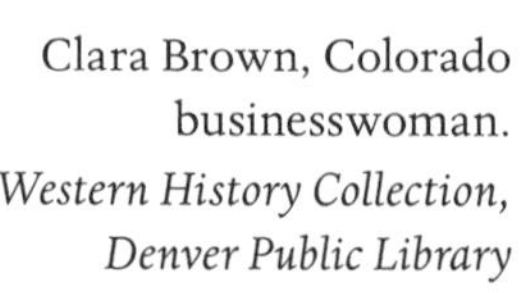

Clara Brown, Colorado businesswoman.
Western History Collection, Denver Public Library

Clara bartered her passage to Colorado in exchange for work. The only African American in the wagon train, she cooked and cared for 26 men (out of 60) during the difficult journey of nearly 700 miles. After eight weeks, the party reached the tiny town of Auraria, a ramshackle collection of buildings, tents, and mud on Cherry Creek, a setup mirrored in the neighboring village of Denver.

Clara quickly found work in a German bakery. A religious and compassionate woman, she plunged into the community's church life and opened her one-bedroom home to prayer meetings. Clara never belonged to any one church but supported the work of all denominations. She began the habit of cooking enough food to feed the hungry and any others down on their luck.

When the bakery owners parted ways, Clara took her washtubs and scrubboard into the mountains to Central City, seeking an even better job opportunity. The mountains' rugged beauty looming against bright blue skies contrasted with the scene below of hacked-down trees, filthy streets, and buildings tottering on stilts meant to keep them from tumbling into the gulches.

Once again, Clara established a laundry business. And oh, did the miners swarming the mountainsides yearn for a handy woman to do their scrubbing and rinsing for them! At fifty cents a shirt—paid in gold dust—and with a thriving business, Brown's earnings grew spectacularly. Ever frugal, she saved every penny not spent on helping others. She also earned income as a midwife. Clara astutely invested her earnings in property and mining shares, amassing a fortune of nearly $10,000—a regal sum. She eventually owned about 16 parcels of land in several places including Central City, Boulder, and Idaho Springs.

Just six months after the end of the Civil War, Clara sold some of these assets to finance a greater project: finding Eliza Jane. She could now safely return to Kentucky and search for her daughter. She made the trip east in October 1865, but the journey of her heart's desire ended in disappointment. Clara, however, made the most of her situation—she paid the costs of bringing 16 former slaves back with her to Colorado. The venture cost a great deal of money, and together with losses suffered during fires and floods, and her generosity to others, Brown's fortune dwindled.

But that spirit of charity earned her the respect and gratitude of many in Colorado, a newly minted state of the union in 1876. In the spring of 1879, Clara traveled to Kansas to help African Americans, most of whom were former slaves, who'd flocked west in hopes of a better future. Many were starving, sick, and without resources to begin a new life. Seventy-nine-year-old Clara remained in Kansas through the summer. Central City's newspaper, the *Register,* noted Clara's return in the September 23 issue:

> Aunt Clara Brown, whom everybody in Central knows, returned from a visit to Kansas some few days since, wither she went to look into the condition of the colored refuges and in the interest of the sufferers generally. There are about 5,000 all told. . . . Aunt Clara says they are an industrious and sober class of people who only ask an opportunity to make an honest living.[14]

As Clara entered her 80s, her health began to fail, and she suffered the swellings and shortened breath of congestive heart disease. After Clara's 20 years in Central City, her doctor advised she seek a lower altitude for her health—she should move down the mountains to Denver. The people of Central City and Denver rallied around Clara Brown, raising funds and finding a donated Denver home for her to live in. Then, in the spring of 1881, the Society of Colorado Pioneers, once open only to white men but now expanded to include women, named Clara—a pioneer of 1859—a member.

But the most amazing reward of Clara's long life came in 1882, when she miraculously discovered that her daughter Eliza Jane, lost to Clara at the slave auction 50 years before, was living in Council Bluffs, Iowa. It is unclear how Clara discovered her daughter's whereabouts, but the two reunited in March 1882. Local newspapers reported the amazing story.

Clara died a few years later in October 1885. The Society of Colorado Pioneers summed up Clara's Brown's achievements in a eulogy: "the kind old friend whose heart always responded to the cry of distress, and who, rising from the humble position of slave to the angelic type of a noble woman, won our sympathy and commanded our respect."[15]

Bethenia Owens-Adair

Female Physician

"The regret of my life up to the age of thirty-five," wrote Bethenia Owens-Adair, "was that I had not been born a boy, for I realized very early in life that a girl was hampered and hemmed in on all sides simply by the accident of sex."[16] Over the course of her life, Bethenia challenged her family and neighbors' notions about the proper place of a woman and carved her own path to success.

Dr. Bethenia Owens-Adair.
Oregon Historical Society

One of nine children, Bethenia traveled to Oregon with her parents as a toddler in 1843. She spent her girlhood helping her mother raise the younger children, "for children did not remain babies long when other babies came along so fast and crowded them out of the cradle." Small and mighty, Bethenia worked hard at her chores, craved the outdoors, and with a rebellious streak, earned a reputation as a "tom-boy."

By age 14, in 1854, she'd had only a smattering of education, attending "three months' school in our neighborhood." That year, Bethenia married Legrand Hill, and with help from her parents, the young couple set up housekeeping in a 12-by-14-foot log cabin, stocked with quilts and sheets she'd sewn herself.

Even before the April 1856 birth of their son, George, Bethenia's practical nature recognized Legrand's "want of industry and perseverance." Her husband frittered away time, often delving into trading and speculating, and losing money. The marriage eroded, hastened by Legrand's treatment of George, whom he spanked "unmercifully." When her angry husband threw the little boy on the bed one day, Bethenia left him. At 18, she returned to her parents' home, broken in spirit and health, marked by the disgrace of her failed marriage. "It seemed to me now that I should never be happy or strong again," she wrote. The stigma of divorce "would cling to me all my future life, and sickly babe of two years in my arms, all rose darkly before me."

Barely able to read and write, Bethenia plunged into a whirlwind of self-improvement. While her mother watched George, Bethenia rose early to milk cows and help with washing, ironing, and housework before heading to school with her younger siblings. She progressed quickly in her reading and studies, and in the fall of 1859, with her divorce decree final and her maiden name restored, she "felt like a free woman," she confided. "The world began to look bright once more."

Bethenia turned down her father's offers to help. She worked any job—sewing, nursing, and washing—to support herself and her son. She made arrangements to teach school at a little church over a summer. Out of her 16 students, three were more advanced than Bethenia. She smuggled their books home at night, preparing the next day's lessons with the help of her brother-in-law, "and they never suspected my incompetency," she noted.

Bethenia used her savings to further her own education in Astoria, settling into a hotel with George and a nephew, her board paid by her sister in exchange for six months of work. But her entrance exams placed her in the primary classes—a great embarrassment to Bethenia, as she recited lessons with children as young as eight. By the end of nine months, she'd passed into the advanced classes, mostly by hard work, poring over her books until the small hours of the morning. "Nothing was permitted," she wrote, "to come between me and this, the greatest opportunity of my life."

The next few years brought Bethenia success as a milliner and dressmaker. When a new business threatened her livelihood, she traveled to San Francisco and trained with the best milliner in town, and then returned home to booming business with the latest fashions at her fingertips. Her hard work paved the way for financial freedom and the chance to continue her dream of furthering her education. When she placed George in college in 1870 at the University of California, Berkeley, she expanded her business to include nursing—and found she possessed a gift for doctoring. Studying a borrowed a copy of *Gray's Anatomy*, a medical book, Bethenia spun a new dream, a new goal to chase: Bethenia Owens, doctor.

Spurred by her quest, Bethenia spent an entire year planning and saving before traveling to Philadelphia to enter the Eclectic School of Medicine. Only eclectic and homeopathic schools routinely allowed women students. Eclectic medicine offered treatments based on gentler remedies and plant-based medicines; they were alternatives to the harsh medical practices of bleeding, purging, and dosing patients with dangerous ingredients like mercury. Bethenia settled in, hired a tutor, attended clinics and lectures at a nearby hospital, and studied like a woman possessed.

After graduation, Bethenia returned to her hometown of Roseburg, Oregon, and found people viewed her as an oddity, or worse—a pushy woman not content to stay near home and hearth. The six male physicians in town tried to embarrass her with an invitation to an autopsy. The autopsy involved male genital organs, and any modest female would decline the viewing. Bethenia answered their stares by stating that one part of the human body should be as sacred to the physician as another. She stayed put. One doctor threatened to leave if a female remained present at a male autopsy. Bethenia countered that it was no different than a male doctor overseeing the autopsy of a woman. With a last stab at sending her from the room, the physicians asked Bethenia to perform the dissection. Bethenia stepped up to the table and began the autopsy. Afterward, as news of the event spread, people treated her with disgust, shock, and a sense that something scandalous had occurred. Public reaction and hostility drove Bethenia to leave Roseburg and, with her sister, move to Portland.

In Portland, Bethenia ran a practice that offered traditional treatment alongside new ones—such as electrical and medicated baths. George entered medical school, and Bethenia made good money in her practice. But she longed for further education at a regular medical college. In September 1878, she again made the long journey to Philadelphia, hoping to enter the Jefferson Medical College. But the school would not admit female students. Bethenia was advised to try the University of Michigan's medical school; she earned acceptance and studied 16 hours a day for the next nine months. In June 1880, Bethenia Owens graduated, a "full-fledged University Physician of the old school."

For the next six months, Bethenia worked in Chicago, immersing herself in hospital and clinic work. She then gave herself a gift—a trip to Europe, traveling with her son and two fellow female physicians, where they toured the great cities and Bethenia bought state-of-the-art medical instruments to use in her new practice back in Oregon.

For years, Bethenia claimed she was married to her work, and that was fine by her. But at an Oregon's women's suffrage meeting, she met an old friend, John Adair. The two married in July 1884 and later shared a great joy when, at age 47, Bethenia had a baby daughter. But the baby died a few days after birth, leaving Bethenia inconsolable. She agreed to move to a more remote farm where she soon began providing medical care for her far-flung neighbors. Called out day or night, she traveled to patients on foot and horseback, through mud and swollen streams and howling winds. In 1891, she and John adopted a boy and named him after his father.

After 11 years of farm work and doctoring, the couple moved to North Yakima, Washington. But Bethenia felt her skills had languished buried on the farm, a move she came to regret. Soon she returned to school, earning a postgraduate degree at the Chicago Clinical School.

As Bethenia grew older, she tired of balancing her medical practice with the wifely demands of her household duties. Her solution proved simple—she gave up the housework. Hitting her stride again, Bethenia kept to her busy schedule, rising early for a cold bath and exercise. She retained the satisfaction of having a large medical practice until her retirement in 1905.

Bethenia also nurtured her health and political interests through her efforts for women's voting rights, the Women's Christian Temperance Union, and her push for more exercise and shorter skirts for women. She refuted the notion that woman should only ride a horse sidesaddle, instead of astride, the way a man rode. "Nothing will preserve a woman's grace . . . so much as vigorous . . . exercise, and horse-back riding stands at the head of the list, provided," Bethenia urged, a woman have "a foot in each stirrup, instead of having the right limb twisted around a [saddle] horn, and the left foot in a stirrup twelve or fifteen inches above where it ought to be."

Bethenia Owens-Adair died on September 11, 1926, at a fine old age that had seen her blaze her own trail. She went from an illiterate girl, married at 14, to a well-educated and respected female physician in the Old West, and she'd earned every bit of that respect through her own hard work and determination.

4
AND NOW THE FUN BEGINS

"Buffalo Gals won't you come out tonight and dance by the light of the moon."

—Lyrics from "Buffalo Gals," a popular 19th-century song

For decades, the West suffered from a great female shortage. In the first years of western expansion, explorers, mountain men, and fur traders contentedly married Native American, Mexican, and Spanish women. A fur trader found his Indian wife's wilderness know-how and tanning skills, as well as the help of her family, invaluable to his business. In California, New Mexico, and Texas, American businessmen and merchants often married into Spanish families. Some men married women from well-to-do families, acquiring citizenship, thousands of acres of land, and business contacts. But the majority of males wed Mexican women from less affluent families; the white husband often raised his wife's family's status and prosperity.

One man waxed poetic on the charms of Mexican women for "their small feet, finely turned ankles, well-developed busts, small and classically formed hands, dark and lustrous eyes, teeth of beautiful shape and dazzling whiteness, and hair of that rich and jetty blackness . . . they are joyous, sociable, kind-hearted creatures."[1] An English visitor arrogantly assured his fellows that Mexican women despised "their own countrymen" and would not hesitate to share their lives with "the dashing white hunters who swagger in all their towns."[2]

Mexican women in California, 1850s. *Library of Congress*

But as increasing numbers of white women arrived west, racial prejudices influenced white men to reject Indian and Hispanic women as suitable wives. Though in high demand, white females arrived in low numbers compared to the eager multitude of single men. A mining camp woman recalled that in two years she'd seen only one other white woman. "Men on all sides," she reported, "but none but Indian women."[3]

Male settlers in Oregon and Washington territories advertised for brides in Eastern newspapers. In Oregon a man and his wife could each claim 320 acres of free land. The demand for brides rose dramatically. Widows remarried within months. Wealthy women hired homely female servants, hoping they wouldn't attract husbands of their own. But they still saw their maids and cooks snatched up on the marriage market at great speed.

For women stuck in unhappy marriages, the odds of finding a better spouse seemed bright. One mining camp woman wrote news which probably shocked her sister back east:

> I tell you the women are in great demand in this country no matter whether they are married or not. You need not think strange if you see me coming home with some good looking man some of these times . . . it is all the go here for Ladys to leave their Husbands two out of three do it there is a first rate chance for a single woman she can have her choice of thousands.[4]

A few women commented that the scarcity of "proper females" forced men to behave in a more chivalrous manner. "A woman on the frontier," claimed Elizabeth Custer, "is so cherished and appreciated, because she has the courage to live out there."[5] Luzena Wilson recalled with humor:

> Every man thought every woman in that day a beauty. Even I have had men come forty miles over the mountains, just to look at me, and I never was called a handsome woman, in my best days, even by my most ardent admirers.[6]

Kick Up Your Heels

Dancing, a beloved entertainment on the frontier, suffered during the female shortage. Three hundred men and a mere 12 women attended the first dance held in Nevada City, California. A few of the men tied bandanas around their arms and assumed the role of "ball-room belles" for the evening.

Dances in towns, large settlements, and army posts featured bands, decorations, and ball gowns. But people also kicked up their heels at dances held in schools, barns, livery stables, courthouses, and on cleared patches of land. In more intimate settings, people might shove furniture against the walls and dance in a home, with a single fiddle player providing music. Sometimes, without any instrumental music, folks danced, clapped, and sang popular tunes like "Skip to My Lou." A good dance lasted till morning light, with refreshments served at midnight, before weary revelers trekked as many as 30 or 40 miles back home after breakfast.

Theater proved another popular form of Western entertainment—a female onstage usually guaranteed a packed house. Cities like San Francisco and Denver boasted glittering theaters and famous talent. Fights among the customers might be more interesting than the performances, however, if the stage meant a few boards and a blanket for a curtain hung up at the back of a saloon.

Actresses willing to travel to the mining camps earned bags of gold and silver for their troubles. Miners showed up in droves to watch their favorites. Mysterious Lola Montez performed her notorious spider dance, an excuse to "kick high and shake her petticoats" claimed one observer. Caroline Chapman's repertoire included Shakespearean drama and musical comedy, as well as a spoof of Montez. A petite redhead named Lotta Crabtree charmed audiences as a child with her spirited mandolin playing, singing, and dancing. She later conquered fans in the East and Europe.

Known as the Frenzy of Frisco, Adah Isaacs Menken thrilled audiences with her hit play *Mazeppa*. The scandalous climactic scene featured Menken strapped to the back of a horse wearing

Adah Isaacs Menken in a series of daring photographs. *Library of Congress*

a flesh-colored body suit and tights. Menken earned more than $100,000 worth of gold, silver, and jewels for a single performance before the miners of Virginia City, Nevada. "A magnificent spectacle dazzled my vision," wrote young reporter Sam Clemens (later known as Mark Twain) when Menken appeared in San Francisco in 1863. "The whole constellation of the Great Menken came flaming out of the heavens," he wrote, "and shed a glory abroad as it fell! I have used the term 'Great Menken' because I regard it as a more modest expression than the 'Great Bare.'"[7]

The details of Menken's early life remain murky, but she was most likely born in Louisiana as Ada Bertha Theodore to a mixed-race mother and a Jewish father in 1835. Her five marriages, including one to a heavyweight boxing champion, and numerous lovers added to her mystique. As a follower of Rabbi Isaac Wise, father of Reform Judaism, Menken learned Hebrew (she spoke several other languages, as well) and wrote poetry and essays for the *Israelite*, a newspaper. When questioned if she'd been born a Jew, Menken told a reporter, she was "born in that faith [Judaism], and have adhered to it through all my erratic career. Through that pure and simple religion I have found greatest comfort and blessing."[8]

Menken died in Paris in 1868, at age 33, probably of tuberculosis. The disease killed many and carried the more genteel 19th-century label of "consumption," as it was a disease that consumed the lungs.

"Got Me a New Calico Dress"

With their lives requiring simple work clothes sewn from durable fabrics, Western women often claimed they cared not a bit for fashion. Living so far from big Eastern cities, everyone wore out-of-date dresses. But in truth, Western ladies appreciated a bit of finery and saved it for special occasions. Even women buried on remote homesteads devoured Eastern magazines like *Godey's Lady's Book* from cover to cover, seeking new ideas to update their wardrobe in the latest styles. "Because I must wear calico," asked one Kansas woman, "must I also be deprived of the pleasure of admiring the beautiful attire of my more fortunate sisters?"[9]

Another Kansas woman defended the image of Western women. "People are generally . . . not half so heathenish as many imagine," she penned to her local paper. "People expect taste and tidiness in dress, at least in ladies, just as much as in the East."[10] Mail-order businesses shipped yards of ribbons, lace, and braid to Western homesteads, and a woman might transform a dress by adding a bit of trim or refashioning the sleeves. And a new Chinese silk shawl or scarf arriving at California ports instantly brightened an old outfit.

The era of Western settlement coincided with the age of hoop skirts, wire-cage bustles, heavy petticoats, and waist-pinching corsets that encased women from armpits to hips. Helen Carpenter wrote from the California Trail in June 1857 about the hoop skirt fashion pushing west:

> There is a bride & groom in the Inman party. The bride wears hoops. We have read of hoops being worn, but they had not reached Kansas before we left so these are the first we've seen and would not recommend them for this mode of traveling. In asides the bride is called "Miss Hoopy."[11]

Elizabeth Custer's hoop skirts measured five yards around the bottom, and the plains wind, gusting beneath the huge bell of her skirt, caused a few embarrassing moments. To outwit the elements, she sewed strips of lead into her dress hems, and "thus loaded down, we took our constitutional [walk] about the post."[12]

Susan Magoffin found Mexican women's dress rather shocking. Writing from New Mexico in 1846, she noted "the women were clad in chemises and petticoats only,"[13] which Susan wore as undergarments. Martha Summerhayes, an army wife, however, soon admired the sensible clothing of Mexican women who left their arms bare and wore scooped necklines and ankle-exposing skirts in the Southwestern heat. But at her husband's insistence, Martha sweltered in high-necked, long-sleeved dresses, like any well-bred woman back east in the 1870s. And no white woman, laced into her steel- or whale-boned corset beneath pounds of clothing, would dream of donning the loose-fitting, though quite modest, dresses of Native American women.

Some women experimented with feminist Amelia Bloomer's new costume—a below-the-knee-length dress worn over baggy, ankle-length pants that were quickly dubbed bloomers. Miriam Colt found the Bloomer dress,

> well suited to a wild life like mine. Can bound over the prairies like an antelope, and am not in so much danger of setting my clothes on fire while cooking when these prairie winds blow. . . . I would not submit myself to wearing long dresses, when I can go so nimbly around . . . to bring water, pick up chips, bring in wood, milk.[14]

But even with the danger of setting oneself on fire, most women said "no thanks" to the bold Bloomer costume, which many scorned as unfeminine. When one girl wore her father's pants to do chores, her brothers hooted with laughter, but her mother was angry. Had her daughter lost her last shred of dignity in the Western wilds?

A ranch woman described the evolution of her riding wear. For ten years she politely rode sidesaddle, dressed in a feminine riding habit with fitted bodice and long flowing skirt. Slowly, her outfit changed. She added a blue flannel shirt, followed by blue denim knickers under a shorter split blue denim skirt. "Decadence having set in," she reported, "the descent from the existing standards of female modesty to purely human comfort and convenience was swift."[15]

For the most part, frontier women clung to fashion tradition, even if a year or two outdated, as a means of validating their womanhood and adding a quiet sheen of civilization to their rough lives.

"The Neighborhood All Turns Out"

No matter their lack of high-fashion identity, Western women created busy social lives for themselves as soon as possible. Women living in towns, large or small, accomplished this with more ease than isolated females. Town ladies even kept up such social graces as formal visits and afternoon tea. People gathered for card parties, cribbage, and evenings of music.

Women on farms and ranches created reasons to visit far-flung neighbors, helping one another with chores, joining in quilting bees and wool-carding parties, or establishing sewing circles. Keturah Belknap hated to pick over her wool alone, so she invited over a dozen ladies and finished the job off in a day. "I have had my party," she wrote. "They seemed to enjoy themselves fine. [We] had a fine chicken dinner. For cake I made a regular old fashioned pound cake like my mother used to make . . . and now my name is out as a good cook so I am alright, for good cooking makes good friends."[16]

Bachelors, on their best behavior, congregated at women's houses to dine, listen to music, and play games—they lapped up the comforts of a female-kept home. One mining-town woman reported, "Had a spirited evening. It was exciting to meet two new gentlemen both good looking and interesting. . . . Talked of books."[17] On a different night, at a different house, "The jest ran high and the laughter loud. Had some good refreshments and returned home."[18]

Neighbors gathered at barn raisings, harvest parties, or corn-husking bees to share work and then dancing and good food. In the Pacific Northwest, people met for clamming parties at the shore. Winter snow called plains pioneers outdoors for sleighing and skating. Spring and summer brought berry picking, croquet, and picnics.

Folks trekked many miles for special celebrations. The Fourth of July was a favorite holiday in the West, crammed with horse races, picnics, speeches, parades, dances, and fireworks. Depending on the customs and traditions of a settler's heritage, a wedding might be a small gathering at home or a full-blown, several-day party with suppers, songs, and dancing. Crowds assembled for yearly events like Court Day or political meetings. Women often spent days baking hundreds of pies and cakes for these occasions.

Churches offered Westerners a chance to socialize and feel part of a community. "I can see all the neighbors twice a week," confided one woman, "for we have prayer meeting Thursday evenings." People longed for the familiar habits of life back east, and building a church represented an important step. Many Western settlements, however, did not have enough families or money to support churches; instead settlers looked forward to the arrival of a traveling preacher.

Camp meetings, which lasted for days, involved preaching, singing, and conversions to the faith. People traveled from miles around and camped out to be part of the worship and

A picnic beneath a cactus in Arizona, 1886. *National Archives*

social excitement. One Oregon woman hosted a 10-day prayer meeting at her house. "Our one room," she wrote, "served for church, kitchen, dining room, bedroom, and study for the preachers, sometimes we had three or four as they came from adjoining circuits to help us through the week."[19] Wrote another woman, "We looked forward to the camp meeting in June. . . . I think they were pretty nearly our only salvation from entire stagnation."[20]

Quiet Moments

With so much daily work, women also enjoyed quiet pastimes, meditative moments to themselves. Writing letters, scribbling in diaries, playing instruments, singing, and embroidering all offered solace and relaxation. Women read and reread, loaned and borrowed books, magazines, and newspapers. All across the frontier, book-hungry women joined literary societies to share books and ideas and listen to guest speakers. With few books available, women set aside money to order reading materials through the mail. Army wives commented on their "precious books," while a South Dakota woman confided, "Seeing the end of my book approaching was like eating the last bit of food on my plate, still hungry, and no more food in sight."[21]

Most Western women embraced the climate and Western winds. They enjoyed horseback riding, fishing, and hunting. Some even tackled mountain climbing. Women studied plants and animals and recorded their findings through photographs and drawings. During the 1870s, Colorado's Martha Maxwell gained a national reputation as a taxidermist and zoologist.

In all areas of the West, women sought joy in life to match their hard work. They often discovered fun in simple things and nothing more than friendly company.

Martha Dartt Maxwell

Colorado Naturalist

In May 1860, after a monotonous month "journeying over a sea of land," Martha Maxwell caught her first faint glimpse of Colorado's Rocky Mountains far in the distance. "We saw them looming up silvery and beautiful," she wrote, "in the robes of eternal white. . . . They appear more & more magnificent each day."[22] Martha's love affair with the natural world—plants and animals and science—turned passionate in the Colorado beauty.

Hoping to recoup the family finances in Colorado's gold mines, Martha and her husband, James, had left their home and young daughter, Mabel, in Baraboo, Wisconsin, and migrated to Colorado. Like many hopefuls, they passed through Denver and headed into the surrounding mining camps, typically places of squalor surrounded by majestic peaks and open blue skies. And like many women, Martha buckled down to the hard work of running a laundry and hotel to keep the family afloat.

Martha's independent streak had been born and bred in Pennsylvania and then Wisconsin by a family that encouraged learning. Martha attended one year of college at Oberlin in Ohio before a lack of money shut down her education. But she'd loved the atmosphere of learning, singing in the choir, and attending lectures on social issues like temperance and abolition. Reluctantly back in Wisconsin, she turned to teaching—one of the few professions open to women—despairing that she would never be able to continue her own education.

Then, in August 1853, local businessman James Maxwell offered Martha an opportunity to return to college. A widower

Martha Maxwell poses with some of her taxidermy specimens.
Denver Public Library, Western History Collection

with six children, Maxwell asked Martha to serve as a chaperone—while taking classes—for his daughter, Emma, and son, James, at Lawrence University in Appleton, Wisconsin. Martha spent a busy year at Lawrence tending to the Maxwell children, studying, working on the university's literary journal, and joining the Young Ladies Mutual Improvement Association.

Then James Maxwell threw Martha a curveball: he desired a suitable person to marry. Would Martha be interested? "I like you," he wrote, "not because I think you handsome, above many, neither because I think you have gifts or graces, natural or acquired above many, but because I think you have good, warm, affections, with a sound judgment and discretion."[23] Hardly the proposal a young woman hoped for. He hoped the 20-year difference in their ages would not matter.

For more than a month, a blanket of silence greeted James's letter. He wrote again, and this time Martha answered, questioning whether she could manage the responsibility of mothering his six children. She also did not want to repay his kindness to her by joining into a relationship, "which might, I fear, secure to you misery instead of happiness."[24] In the end, however, 22-year-old Martha Dartt relented and married James Maxwell on March 30, 1854.

Throughout the 1850s, Martha managed the family home and crusaded for causes. Just a few months after her marriage, she joined a temperance raid on local taverns, pouring bottles of liquor onto the floor in an event dubbed the Whiskey War of 1854. A justice of the peace let Martha go after her husband agreed to pay for damages. Martha also worked to support the free-state faction in Kansas, those opposed to allowing slavery to enter the territory.

In November 1857, Martha gave birth to her only child, a daughter named Mabel. But during these years, a bad economy, coupled with poor money decisions, eroded the family finances. News headlines heralding the 1859 gold strikes in Colorado spurred the Maxwells, along with thousands of others, west to the Rockies.

The rough conditions in the mining camps allowed Martha a degree of independence. And she had something to prove. "You know some of my Baraboo friends were inclined to laugh at me for coming out here," she wrote her sisters, "saying that it was no place for a woman and that I would be only a bill of expense & a bother."[25]

During the years moving about Colorado, Martha ran a boardinghouse and restaurant, baked, mended and scrubbed clothes, sold pies, and hosted dances and theatricals in the hall she had built. Martha invested in mining claims and eventually bought a small ranch with a one-room log cabin. She also became a founding member of the Nevada City temperance group. The work proved hard and the reward steady (but never very much), and at one point her hard work vanished in a wall of flames that swept through the mining town.

After two and half years, Martha returned to Baraboo—and her long-neglected daughter. Mabel, now five, did not recognize her mother. It set the stage for a lifetime of misunderstanding and tension between Mabel and Martha.

While back in Wisconsin, Martha received an offer of work that changed the path of her life. A professor at the Baraboo Collegiate Institute wanted a collection of mounted birds and animals to form the basis of a department of zoology. Martha had attempted to learn the process of stuffing animals, the art of taxidermy, when she first saw some mounted birds in Colorado. She had written her family, "I wish to learn how to preserve birds & other animal curiosities in this country."[26] Now she threw herself wholeheartedly into this new opportunity.

For the next two years, while James mostly lived in Colorado, Martha learned taxidermy, ran the Maxwell household, and stayed active in Baraboo through organizations like the Loyal Women's League, which aided Union soldiers during the

Civil War. But the work wore Martha out, and her health deteriorated. In September 1866 she entered a sanitarium in Battle Creek, Michigan, to rest and take treatments. The sanitarium promoted good health through a vegetarian diet, water cures, fresh air and light, sleep, and rest. But if Martha did not mind the separation from James, the distance from Mabel did hurt.

Martha returned to Baraboo in the spring of 1867, but not for long. She packed up Mabel and headed to an idealistic society recently founded in Vineland, New Jersey. Feminists, temperance people, and reformers flocked here. Edward Everett Hale, speaker and author, reported Vineland was the only place he'd visited where "I have found the greater part of the women satisfied."[27] But this time, Martha's quest for independence had gone too far. James asked Martha to return to Colorado. She refused. He traveled east, and in short order, James, Martha, and Mabel headed to Colorado.

Back in the Rockies, settling in the Boulder area, Martha pursued her passion for the natural world and taxidermy. At first she relied on local boys or James to furnish her with bird and animal specimens for mounting. But this proved unreliable. Martha practiced her marksmanship and soon toted her own gun into the mountains on collecting expeditions, often traveling with James, Mabel, and Martha's sister, Mary. Not cold, rain, or rocky slopes could prevent Martha from collecting birds and mammals of every size. Carting the animals back to Boulder for preparation proved an arduous task. Then Martha began the heavy and often unpleasant work of skinning the animals, building a support structure, and recreating the creatures to lifelike affect.

In October 1868, Martha presented a display of her work at the Colorado Agricultural Society. Reported the *Rocky Mountain News*, "The largest collection of Colorado birds we have ever seen is now on exhibition at the Fair Grounds. They were picked up by Mrs. Maxwell, of Boulder, within six months, count over 100 different kinds, and are arranged on two large shrubs of cottonwood with a great deal of taste." The collection did "rare credit to the skill and scientific attainments of the lady."[28]

In an era when society viewed a woman's role as that of nurturer, homemaker, and wife, Martha instead devoted her life to study and work. The times made it nearly impossible for a woman who desired a career to also have a happy marriage.

Martha felt unprepared by her lack of education to carry on the serious work of a naturalist. In early 1869, she wrote to the secretary of the Smithsonian Institution in Washington, DC, asking what books he recommended to study birds. "I am making a collection of Colorado specimens," she wrote, "have something over a hundred different varieties, among them are some which seem new and strange, at least I am unable to classify them with my present light upon the subject."[29]

Martha's letter sparked a relationship with the Smithsonian, one of the country's most prestigious seats of science, which lasted for the rest of her life. Over the years, she corresponded regularly with Smithsonian secretary Spencer Baird and ornithologists Robert Ridgway and Elliott Coues. Baird asked Martha to help build up the Smithsonian's collection by sending eggs and nests of Colorado species. She also wrote Baird about the different birds and their habitats, some of which she collected from elevations of nearly 8,000 feet. When Martha discovered a new subspecies of screech owl, Robert Ridgway named it after her (*Otus asio maxwelliae*) "not only as a compliment to an accomplished and amiable lady, but also as a deserved tribute to her high attainments in the study of natural history."[30]

Martha continued her taxidermy work, often to the point of exhaustion. She added to her own collection and mounted animals for others. She again displayed at the Colorado Agricultural Fair—an astounding 600 specimens including wild cats, wolves, deer, antelope, eagles, and reptiles—and won two ten-dollar prizes. But with money always an issue, she ended up selling most of her collection to a botanical garden in Missouri. The sale proved a bitter blow to Martha, who'd worked so hard to create the collection, and the payment of $600 was less than what she'd spent to create the specimens.

With the collection gone, what else could Martha do but begin the laborious process of building it up once again? Clad in her expedition outfit of bloomers under a calf-length skirt, Martha collected the birds, animals, and reptiles she needed. James seemed happy to accompany his wife on her trips. Back home in her "den," she devoted all her energy to work. Her sister Mary commented, "Society was ignored, all superfluous articles of food and dress were dispensed with."[31] Mabel noted that her mother was never at home; if she was, she remained consumed in her work. Writing years later, as an old woman of 90, Mabel recalled, "I was bitterly jealous of the animals that seemed to absorb all the interest and affection for which I longed."[32]

The den contained the tools of Martha's trade and art. Piles of hemp, cotton, hay, and wire lay about. Branches of trees, bars of iron, brushes, paints, and putty covered surfaces. Bottles of insects and reptiles, nests and eggs, shells, glass eyes, bones, antlers, and skins lined the shelves. Martha carefully measured each animal to build an artificial body, and over it she stretched and fit the skin. She cleaned and preserved bones, studied the shape of skeletons and muscle and sinew. She often used the leg bones to mount the animal and a body shaped from iron with stuffing of cotton or wool. Martha, in remote Colorado, and pretty much self-taught in taxidermy, was using techniques that were several years ahead of her time.

Martha also perfected the art of displaying her specimens in naturalistic settings and poses, such as baby birds in a nest, their necks stretched and beaks open, as their mother (with a rabbit in her talons) hangs over them. Martha seemed to work almost frantically; the family always needed money, and she worried about paying for Mabel's college education.

In June 1874, Martha opened a new educational and moneymaking venture—the Rocky Mountain Museum in Boulder. She hoped the museum would serve as a scientific institution and work in harmony with the new state university. She hoped that her exhibits, "if artistically mounted and arranged, would interest the young, and awaken in them a love" for the natural world. She also featured "curiosities" meant to entice the paying public. Her vision once again placed her at the front of the scientific and museum world.

The main attractions, alongside the fossils, minerals, antique coins, and Indian pieces, were Martha's specimens. A huge buffalo dominated the center of the room. Birds perched in treetops. A doe licked her two fawns. A bear crawled out of a cave. A mountain lion sprang through the branches of a tree. People gawked and wondered. Critics and the public loved it. Newspapers in the East even took note. But the museum could not sustain itself. Martha eventually moved her museum to Denver, where she again found little success. At this low point, however, she received an offer that could lift her talents to new heights.

The United States prepared to celebrate the nation's centennial with a huge exhibition in Philadelphia. The men in charge of Colorado's exhibit asked Martha to crate her animals and create a display honoring the state's wildlife. Ten million visitors would pass through the exhibition halls and pavilions with Martha's groundbreaking creation dazzling them as one of the top draws.

Arriving in Philadelphia in the spring of 1876, Martha worked round the clock with an assistant to build a Rocky Mountain fantasy using paste, pulverized ore, lime, gravel, evergreens, and water. The display was breathtaking—stones, trees, a stream, a lake, the plains. It had every manner of bird, fish, mammal, and reptile—huge buffalo and elk, bears, mountain sheep, turtles, fish, rattlesnakes, and more. A placard on the front of the exhibit proclaimed this all to be WOMAN'S WORK.

Martha intended that her efforts prove something. "The greatest desire of my life," she had written to Spencer Baird the year before, "is to help inspire women with confidence in their own resources and abilities. Talk is pure nonsense, about the matter, work, and excellence in the things wrought, will set the whole matter right."[33]

Martha's exhibit amazed people. Some poked the animals, insisting they must be alive. Visitors bombarded Martha with questions. Had she killed the animals herself? How had she stuffed them? Was the game really this thick in Colorado? Everyone was crazy for information about Colorado. One of the Colorado commissioners noted that Martha's collection actually brought people to the exhibit as word spread—"her fame increased every day to the last week and the last day."[34]

Articles about Martha Maxwell and her display appeared in magazines like *Harper's Bazaar*, while newspaper articles popped up everywhere, even as far away as Paris. Martha herself proved fascinating. People marveled that a tiny woman, less than five feet tall, a "modest," "refined," and "delicate" woman, could have done such hard labor.

As to questions about how she could kill the animals, Martha had a plain answer. "There isn't a day you don't tacitly consent to have some creature killed that you may eat it. I never take life for such carnivorous purposes! All must die some time; I only shorten the period of consciousness that I may give their forms perpetual memory and I leave it to you, which is the more cruel? to kill to eat, or to kill to immortalize?"[35]

After Philadelphia, however, Martha Maxwell's hope for financial ease based on her success fell through. Colorado failed to pay her the costs for shipping the collection to Philadelphia. She couldn't find a buyer to purchase the collection. With Mabel now in college, Martha frantically sought ways to raise money. She spent the next two summers exhibiting the collection in the East, again claiming critical and scientific success. She tried to make money selling photographs of the display, but the company that owned the rights to sell the images barred her from continuing her own sales.

When Mabel proposed dropping out of school to save the cost, a horrified Martha urged her to stay. "Ever since you were born it has been my ambition to realize in you my own disappointed hopes for education and usefulness. So long as there is the least probability for success," she wrote her daughter, "I cannot give it up."[36] At the same time James Maxwell, who also wanted Mabel to receive an education, warned his daughter that no amount of book learning could atone for a lack of good housekeeping skills, the very foundation of a good home, and something that Martha had failed at.

Martha spent the next few years traveling and exhibiting her work in Washington, DC; Boston; and Philadelphia. With her sister Mary, Martha wrote a book of her experiences, again hoping to reap financial security. But after several years of writing *On the Plains, and Among the Peaks; or, How Mrs. Maxwell Made Her Natural History Collection*, the book, though highly praised, failed to sell. It did create a lasting record of Martha Maxwell's scientific achievements and included catalogs of Martha's work by Ridgway and Coues—who credited Martha with discovering not only a new owl but a black-footed ferret as well.

By 1878, Martha's health was declining. She missed her daughter and struggled with Mabel's different view of women's place in the world. For a while she enrolled in classes at the Woman's Laboratory of the Massachusetts Institute of Technology (MIT). Martha loved school, "but ah me!" she wrote Mary, "it cost lots of money."[37] She gave taxidermy lessons and lived in an attic room like a pauper.

Ill health and hard work marred Martha's last years. At one point, she worked dressing dolls for Christmas sales, commenting to Mary that the dolls "all represent the 'girl of the period' and must have the wasp waist—the long trail [*dress train*] and all the fashionable follies which I detest and I can but think that I am cultivating in other women's daughters the love of just those things which I so much deplore in my own."[38] She did all she could to further Mabel's career as a teacher and fretted when Mabel decided to leave teaching for marriage, a step Martha viewed as a loss of freedom. Martha's own marriage had been a disaster, marked by years of separation.

In her last years, Martha pinned her hopes on opening a beachside resort near Long Island that would feature the collection. But ovarian cancer sapped the energy from Martha's once vigorous body. She died in Mabel's arms on May 31, 1881, not quite 50 years old.

Martha Maxwell went to Colorado as a gold seeker, but she found her life's work in the years she spent tramping through the wilds of Colorado to collect and preserve specimens of the natural world. She was the first woman to do so, in a field, like all others, that belonged to men. She helped pioneer lifelike displays of her specimens in a realistic habitat. Her hard work and determination, which only seemed to reward her with financial insecurity, lost her those things that were meant to matter most to a woman of her time—her marriage and her relationship with her child. But in the end, Martha Maxwell accomplished much of what she set out to do—to show that a woman could excel in her chosen field.

Charlotte "Lotta" Crabtree

"Golden Wonder" of the Stage

In 1855, the mining town of Rabbit Creek, California, witnessed the debut of a local performer, Miss Lotta Crabtree. The show opened in a log theater tacked onto a saloon run by Mart Taylor, a one-time strolling actor who dispensed whiskey along with dance and singing lessons. Meaning to cash in on Lotta's talents, Taylor featured his prized pupil clad in green breeches and a hat. Lotta kicked,

Lotta Crabtree.
Library of Congress

twirled, and tapped through an evening of spirited jigs and reels mixed with sentimental Irish ballads. The little redhead's performance tugged the heartstrings of lonely miners, many of them Irish, just as Taylor had planned. After her last bow, Lotta's mother Mary Ann swept up the coins and golden nuggets tossed onto the stage by the grateful miners. Taylor immediately planned a tour through the mining camps, featuring his new sensation. Lotta Crabtree was eight years old.

Born in New York to English parents on November 7, 1847, Lotta traveled to California with her mother in 1852. Her father John, a ne'er-do-well who often abandoned the family, was already in California seeking his riches in gold. Finding only failure, he sent for Mary Ann and Lotta to come west and open a boardinghouse. Lotta made the harrowing journey with her mother by the fastest route available, traveling across Panama, by boat, train, canoe, and mules, to a sailing ship that carried them to the wicked city of San Francisco. The boomtown boasted at least one murder a day and possessed nearly 750 bartenders catering to the thirst of citizens, while a mere 21 ministers attempted to save the souls of gamblers, adventurers, prostitutes, and miners.

What Mary Ann quickly noticed was San Franciscans' love of theater, and children proved a great draw. Kate and Ellen Bateman, only 11 and 9 years old, played Shakespeare. Sue Robinson, a prominent "fairy star," or child actor, could sing, dance, and recite. Mary Ann met the Chapman family, a clan of actors. Caroline Chapman, singer and dancer, was the rage of San Francisco.

Audiences believed in a long night of entertainment punctuated with variety—Shakespeare, comedies, singing and dancing, minstrel shows, and hand-painted travelogues that slowly unrolled panoramas to narration. The town boasted a number of theaters, some impressive indeed, seating several thousand guests, with lush drapery, gilt domes and columns, and thick carpets. The clientele might still be a little rough, however, and brawling often took place in the aisles even as the show went on. Mary Ann found the possibilities for riches exciting, even if she disapproved of the theater's light morals and scandals.

Once Mary Ann and Lotta hooked up again with John Crabtree in Grass Valley and later Rabbit Creek, Mary Ann enrolled Lotta in dancing and singing lessons. The Crabtrees met Lola Montez, an entertainer with a shady past that included numerous marriages. Montez took an interest in Lotta and encouraged the family's hopes for their daughter's stage career.

After Lotta's debut, she headed off into the mountains with Taylor, her mother, and her baby brother John. Often traveling without road or path, skirting cliffs and boulders, Lotta made the journey strapped to a horse for safety. The group stopped at every two-bit mining town, where Taylor would rent a room. It was sometimes little more than a tent, with sawhorses and boards making a stage and blankets hung in place of a stage curtain. Taylor told jokes and sang and danced, but Lotta stole the show. The evening's take depended upon the miners' luck, and the tour—marred by uneven pay, fear of robbers, and even Indians—continued through dozens of mining camps and scrubby towns.

It wasn't long before Lotta turned into the Crabtree family breadwinner. With Mary Ann pregnant again, Lotta's father even handed his daughter over to another troupe of performers to keep the money flowing. Mary Ann had to send a sheriff to retrieve her daughter from the actors and escort the girl to friends who'd watch Lotta until after the birth of her new brother, George. By 1856, the family pulled together again and headed back to San Francisco.

The theater scene in San Francisco now drew even European musicians and famous Shakespearean actors from the East, like

Edwin Booth. Mary Ann left the two little boys with her sister, and with Mart Taylor accompanied Lotta on several more tours of area mining camps. Miners went wild for Lotta; adopting her as a "pet," they carried her around on their shoulders and sang her out of town when she left.

Lotta expanded her roles by joining a popular minstrel show, playing the character of Topsy from *Uncle Tom's Cabin* in blackface. She perfected her dances and mastered a large collection of songs, comedy bits, and sketches. But in San Francisco, Lotta was only one performer among many, and the town's leading manager and owner of the Opera House Theater, Tom Maguire, failed to book her for his shows.

Instead, Lotta played at the Gaieties, a small theater, in front of a grimy crew of miners, gamblers, and rowdy boys. Most of the entertainment was risqué by 1850s standards. Lotta's sentimental innocence at the end of the show encouraged the audience to reach deep in their pockets and shower the stage with money. But they were tough crowds. In one incident, when a fight drowned out Lotta's young voice, Mary Ann whisked her off the stage to safety.

In performances like this, "La Petite Lotta" paid her dues. For the next few years, Lotta dutifully toured the mining camps and performed all around San Francisco—at amusement parks and markets, at auction houses and low-rent theaters like melodeons where no decent woman would go. But Mary Ann kept order, at least around Lotta. The girl began performing plays, too, not just variety show performances. They were hard years, and while Mary Ann managed the money, it was Lotta's work and long hours that supported the family.

Lotta gained only a smattering of formal education during her childhood—nothing interfered with her moneymaking potential. Her longest stretch of continuous education was only six months. But she studied hard to hone her performing crafts, continuing singing and dancing lessons and learning to play the banjo and mandolin. Lotta possessed that spark of performing that couldn't be taught, however; her natural, often impish, humor and energetic manner lit up the stage and made audiences fall in love.

Though well-known, Lotta failed to get bookings in the grand theaters of San Francisco. Then in March 1862, Lotta got her big break. Theaters had an intimate relationship with local volunteer fire departments. The buildings, filled with wood, plaster, and gaslights, frequently went up in flames, and fighting these fires required quick responses. It became customary for theaters to put on benefit shows to raise money for firemen. Every performer was expected to do his or her part on these elaborate evenings of fundraising.

Lotta's performance at the Metropolitan Temple of Drama to benefit the Knickerbocker Engine Company No. 5 drew raves. Invitations poured in for other benefit performances. She danced lively jigs and hornpipes, performed cheeky comedy sketches, and crooned popular songs like, "The Captain with His Whiskers Gave a Sly Wink at Me," a blend of flirting and innocence. "Rally Round the Flag, Boys," where Lotta strutted around the stage in a soldier's uniform, and her sentimental singing of "Dear Mother, I'll Come Home Again" brought down the house. Lotta was the girl to go anywhere and perform her heart out.

Now 16 and a seasoned performer, Lotta caught the attention of actress Adah Menken, already married three times and the toast of California. Menken convinced the family they needed to gamble a bit with Lotta's career. It was time to leave the familiarity of California, and especially San Francisco, and test whether Lotta's charm could translate to the rest of the country. In April 1864, the Crabtrees left for New York after a tearful farewell performance at Maguire's Opera House, where Lotta raked in a $1,500 paycheck for the single night.

But Lotta's rising star crashed in New York. She played to nearly empty theaters, and one critic claimed, "Her style is certainly not intended for a first-class audience, concert halls being her proper stamping ground."[39] The girl from the Golden West was too "brassy" and low class for New York.

The failure hurt Lotta, but one man recognized her appeal. B. F. Whitman booked her into a war play, *The Seven Sisters*, and sent the Crabtrees on tour to Chicago. Here, audiences again loved Lotta, who played five roles, danced, strutted, and played the banjo. She continued a grueling schedule of shows through nearly every town in the Midwest. She played with different actors at most stops and against whatever backdrop a theater possessed. Once again, Lotta Crabtree filled the seats with spectators, and the money rolled in. Mary Ann collected it all and carried it around in a giant satchel. She also began investing her daughter's money in real estate.

Back east, Lotta conquered Boston, performing 19 times in 13 different plays, often taking on as many as six roles in one play. She continued extensive touring in the Midwest and South. She mostly played young girls or boys who were separated from their parents and lived by their wits, triumphing before the final curtain came down. The characters lived in mining camps, in a lighthouse, in a pawn shop, but all turned out well in the end; Lotta's characters found long-lost parents along with fortune and happiness. At five foot two and with glossy red hair, she could easily play a child's role.

After several exhausting years, Lotta agreed to attempt New York again. People had not seen her, but they had heard of her by now. Advertisements praised Lotta as the "western wonder," the "sparkling ingot," and a "sunbeam." This time, she charmed audiences and critics in plays like *Pet of the Petticoats* and *Little Nell and the Marchioness,* which was written especially for Lotta. One critic noted, "for the proprieties . . . and august traditions of the stage, [Lotta] shows a reckless contempt. . . . She says 'Damn it!' with spirit and gusto. The audience . . . likes to hear a woman swear on the stage."[40]

In *Firefly,* Lotta played a scene as a regimental drummer calling troops to arms. With long flourishes and rolls, she built to a crescendo of drumming as the threat of attack neared. She played for nearly two minutes, the pit orchestra silent, while Lotta's drumming filled the theater, calling forth a host of marching men. Civil War veterans rose in the aisles, women cried, and people cheered. Lotta's share of 28 days of shows was nearly $10,000!

As Lotta's fame and wealth grew, her father and brother John often proved an embarrassment—drinking, womanizing, and losing her hard-earned money in shady investments. Mary Ann mostly kept a lid on finances, doling out meager allowances to her family, including Lotta. She also made sure no young men came courting her daughter. Over the years, men pursued Lotta for her money. A few admirers bordered on stalking, forcing Lotta to lament to a reporter, "I do wish that a man of a little sense would admire me for once."[41] She also enjoyed several romantic suitors, including a Russian grand duke, but Lotta Crabtree never married.

In July 1869, Lotta returned to the welcoming arms of San Francisco, a great star coming home. This time the family journeyed with ease on the newly completed transcontinental railroad. Lotta appeared in eight plays before the elite of San Francisco and the miners who traveled from the camps to see their former darling. She performed a farewell benefit in September, and the audience showered the stage with gold coins and even a diamond tiara.

A new play was written for her—*Heart's Ease*—a story of a child taken to California and then abandoned by her English father. Adventures follow, involving revolvers, buried gold, melodrama, dancing, and banjo playing, before Lotta's character reconciles with her father, returns to England, and marries a proper gentleman. The play was a mainstay for Lotta throughout the 1870s when she formed her own acting company and continued touring the nation.

The *New York Times* boasted Lotta had "the face of a beautiful doll and the ways of a playful kitten." Critics used words like "devilish," "mischievous," and "teasing" to describe her. Ardent male admirers unhitched the horses from Lotta's carriage and pulled her through the streets to the theater. She smoked thin black cigars and closed many shows by pulling back the curtain to reveal her slim ankle, a shock and delight to audiences.

Lotta often played street urchins onstage, and she started devoting large sums of money to clothe and feed children in need, raggedy newsboys, hotel bellhops, and homeless children who flocked to the theater to see their champion. By the time she was 20, Lotta grew more involved in using her money for good, a role she would continue for the rest of her life, telling a reporter in 1874, "Charity is what is needed in this world."[42] In 1875 she presented San Francisco with a fountain—a practical gift that supplied water to thirsty horses and people, with four basins and black tin cups chained to the stonework for drinking. The fountain rose 21 feet into the air, capped with medallions marking California life.

Lotta traveled several times to Europe where she studied French, Italian, and painting, which became a lifelong passion. On one voyage, the ship captain pestered her into performing.

Lotta agreed, but only if the evening turned into a benefit for sailors' orphans. Passengers paid up and jammed the ship's saloon, and Lotta performed.

Her first attempt to conquer the British stage in 1883—like her first attempt to conquer New York—fell glaringly flat. The audience hissed, sneered, and hooted, offended by a play in which Lotta portrayed a gypsy pursued by a lecherous English nobleman and poked fun at a Salvation Army hymn. But in the end, Lotta won over British audiences playing Little Nell, loosely based on Charles Dickens's story *The Old Curiosity Shop.* At one point, she pulled a chair to the edge of the stage and sang, accompanying herself on a mandolin, and audiences loved it. The Prince of Wales even attended a performance.

Lotta retired from her stage career at the age of 45 after suffering a fall onstage that fractured a vertebra. Her last season, in 1890 and 1891, earned her $87,000—a huge sum. And after decades of touring, of giving every ounce of herself to her audience, Lotta determined to spend her remaining time traveling, painting, and helping others.

Audiences had turned a bit from her brand of entertaining—the melodramas and rakish comedies, the rags-to-riches stories—to more realistic plays and sophisticated "drawing room" comedies. Lotta had become a star simply because she was Lotta; as one man described it, "The secret of her charm was as hidden as the scent of the rose; it was there—somewhere."[43]

Lotta retired the richest actress in the country and generously donated to charities helping children, animals, and down-on-their luck actors. Lotta paid her last visit to San Francisco in 1915 for the Panama-Pacific International Exposition. On Lotta Crabtree Day, she stood in front of the largest crowd she ever played before, as thousands flocked to greet her. Lotta spoke a few words and then broke down in gratitude and emotion. The crowd chanted her name before they too dissolved into tears.

When Lotta Crabtree died in 1924, she left an estate valued at $4 million to charity. People claiming to be relatives attacked the will. But in the end, Lotta's money went where she wanted it to, and her fortune still helps people today. Her gift to San Francisco, Lotta's Fountain, remains a city landmark, her tribute to the gold rush where a little girl became a shooting star.

5

GREAT EXPECTATIONS FOR THE FUTURE

"That every woman of the age of twenty one years, residing in this Territory, may, at any election . . . cast her vote."
—Wyoming Territory Legislation, December 1869

Like a wildfire driven before the wind, the west grew quickly. Towns with crowded dirt streets and a hodgepodge of hastily nailed-together buildings provided goods and services for miners, cattlemen, and farmers. But danger and violence lurked around every corner. Popular distractions remained rough—bullfights, horse racing, gambling, lynch mob hangings, and plenty of whiskey guzzling. Even a game of billiards in one case involved guns as men propelled the balls with pistol shots and then shot the tops off decanters behind the bar.

Wichita, Kansas, 1874. *Library of Congress*

"In the short space of twenty-four days, we have had murders, fearful accidents, bloody deaths, a mob, whippings, a hanging, an attempt at suicide, and a fatal duel," reported a female resident of a California mining town.[1] Another woman described her grief and shock when the hanging of two men shattered the Sabbath. Women might enjoy the benefits of town life—available goods, theaters, socializing, and job opportunities—but the lawless ways had to change.

In the 19th century, a woman's role meant raising her children, comforting those in need, and providing a home for her husband to retreat from his daily cares. Preserving the "moral values" of society also rested on a woman's shoulders. Fallen women and drink might lead a man to sin, but a good woman saved not only his soul but the soul of her community as well. For the West, the American Missionary Society prescribed:

> We must send no more unmarried men. California needs woman's influence . . . a devoted intelligent woman can do more than two ministers. A shipload of female missionaries would be the greatest blessing California ever had.[2]

In the American East and South, the lives of middle- and upper-class women grew more restrictive during the 1800s. In the view of one male writer, women naturally shrank from the struggle and competition of life. Like a child, he wrote, a woman "has but one right and that is the right to protection. The right to protection involves the obligation to obey."[3] Throughout much of the 19th century, women held no legal right to vote, own property, or gain custody of their children.

Frontier women lacked these rights, too, but they might have laughed at the notion that they shrank from life's struggle. Western women did not sit back demurely and leave the job of settling Western lands to men. There was simply too much to accomplish—often survival itself lay at stake. Women, wrote one from Kansas, "learned at an early age to depend upon themselves to do whatever work there was to be done, and to face danger when it must be faced."[4]

While the West produced its share of notorious ladies like barroom brawler Martha Jane Cannary, better known as Calamity Jane, and the outlaws Pearl Hart and Belle Star, most women who lent a hand settling the frontier were ordinary

Calamity Jane claimed work as a Pony Express rider and an Indian scout. *Library of Congress*

people. Women and men both believed that frontier rawness needed reform. Men, however, could initiate change through their votes and by holding public office. Without political rights, women found other ways to push for change.

As the art of sheer survival gave way to a more settled life, women found important elements missing from the Western scene. If a woman's role was to civilize and hold at bay the darker shades of humanity, she'd begin with those things nearest her heart, and schools and churches stood at the top of the list.

School Is in Session

Many women believed in the power of schools to civilize the rough frontier. When too few families lived in an area to support a school, mothers taught their children at home or sent them to neighbor women for instruction. Lessons included reading, writing, and math, with a good dose of morality thrown in as well. Some Westerners, especially army families, made sacrifices to send their children back east for their education.

As soon as enough school-age children lived in a county, parents banded together to form school systems. Women traveled the county collecting signatures of support for the schools and penned letters to county and state superintendents. Tax money didn't always cover the cost of teachers' pay and schoolhouses, so mothers pitched in to make up shortfalls with fundraisers like box suppers and local theatrical performances. Parents themselves often built the schoolhouse when an existing building or room couldn't be found, and families welcomed teachers into their homes as boarders. One South Dakota woman, a teacher before marriage, felt that "just having a school available made life look a lot better to me."[5]

By organizing schools, many women entered public affairs for the first time. If women helped establish schools and worked in them as teachers, why shouldn't they have a vote on school taxes, bonds, and school board elections? Why shouldn't a woman sit on the school board or be elected superintendent?

Nebraskan Luna Kellie first asked such questions when childless local men tried to cut the length of the school term to save taxes. "Right then," claimed Kelly,

> I saw for the first time that a woman might be interested in politics and want a vote. I had been taught that it was unwomanly to concern oneself with politics and that only the worst class of women would ever vote if they had a chance etc etc but now I saw where a decent mother might wish very much to vote on local affairs at least.[6]

In 1861, Kansas became the first state to allow women to vote in school elections.

Time for Religion

From the days of the Oregon Trail, women deplored the lack of religion in Western life. "And today is Sunday again," mourned a westward-bound female. "O what Sundays. There is nothing that seems like the Sabbath."[7] Women missed the comfort, strength, and community found in religious services. Many feared for their children's well-being, as they had been raised without churches and knew the benefit of traveling ministers' visits only three or four times a year. Bible reading at home could not replace weekly worship with others, they believed.

As they had with schools, women often took the lead in raising funds to build local churches and hire ministers. One woman took three boarders into her home so she might contribute to her community's church-building coffers. Women opened their homes for church services and prayer meetings, taught Sunday school, and oversaw charity work.

Other groups brought their faith to the frontier. Members of the Church of Jesus Christ of Latter-Day Saints, or Mormons, faced persecution in Ohio, Missouri, and Illinois. In 1846–1847, Brigham Young, who led the group after founder Joseph Smith was murdered in 1844, called for a great migration of the group to the valley of the Salt Lake in Utah. In this land no one else wanted, Mormons would build their own Zion.

Mormon women who had trekked across the plains for religious freedom served their church with devotion and supported the Mormon religion throughout the Utah Territory and the West. By the 1860s, thousands of Mormons had settled in the valley, building an irrigation system, ironworks, mills, and a telegraph system. In the heart of Salt Lake City, work began on a temple for worship and a tabernacle that would hold 10,000 people for public gatherings and singing.

Anti-Mormon sentiments, however, ran high in America—"the Mormons must be treated as enemies and exterminated or driven from the state," wrote the governor of Missouri in 1838.[8] Though similar to other Protestants sects, people viewed Mormons as a secret society, set apart. As a theocracy, Mormon leaders ruled both church and state. The Mormon economy, based on shared work and wealth in the early days, clashed with America's spirit of competition and free enterprise.

But what really inspired the public's wrath was polygamy. Joseph Smith had decreed that men had a spiritual duty to marry as many wives as they could support. Less than 20 percent of Mormons actually lived in plural marriages, but journalists and novelists skewered Mormon men as lecherous drunkards who abused their wives and kidnapped girls. They depicted Mormon women as harlots and conniving harpies—insane, stupid, and "debauched" females who failed in their role as moral guardians of society. Writers insisted that Mormon women gave birth to defective children and then neglected and abused them.

Many of the writers describing the evils of Mormon life were women. Novels described scenes of torture and abduction. In florid language, one female novelist detailed the fate of a wife who'd spoken against polygamy: "[She] was taken one night when she stepped out for water, gagged, carried a mile into the woods, stripped nude, tied to a tree, and scourged till the blood ran from her wounds to the ground, in which condition she was left till the next night."[9]

Two Mormon women also wrote books. Ann Eliza Young, Brigham Young's 19th wife, declared, "Incest, murder, suicide, mania, and bestiality are the chief 'beauties' of this infamous system."[10] But Fanny Stenhouse recalled the all-too-real anguish of a first wife accepting her husband's marriage to another woman: "I shrank from the realization that *our* home was at last to be desecrated by the foul presence of Polygamy." She wrote that, on the day of the wedding, "To me their tender tones were daggers piercing my heart and filling me with a desire to revenge myself upon the father of my children." Every day she faced the sight of her husband with another woman "in the midst of my family."[11] Fanny found the situation consuming and unbearable. After a year, her husband built a separate house for the second wife, giving Fanny some relief.

While many Mormon women disliked plural marriages, they defended their moral character and pointed to a Biblical precedent for polygamy. They argued that Mormon women actually gained freedom because of polygamy, as wifely demands were shared. However, under political pressure from the United States, in 1890 the Mormon Church ended the practice of polygamy.

Small numbers of Jewish women also made new homes in the West. Most emigrated from Europe, mainly Bavaria and Poland, to escape religious persecution and economic hardship. Many Western Jews moved not to farms but to towns, like San Francisco, where they stood a better chance of organizing synagogues with other Jewish families and hiring rabbis. Jewish men wanted Jewish brides, and many women came west as part of arranged marriages, their husbands-to-be (whom they had never met) paying their travel to America and the cost of their new outfits.

Family roots in Europe determined social rank in Western Jewish communities. A Polish Jew was denied access to the upper crust of society that welcomed a Jewish woman from Bavaria. Jewish woman strove to maintain strict standards within their households; daughters bathed and "dressed for dinner," and wine was set on the table next to candelabras. As Claire Hofer Hewes recalled of her girlhood in Carson City,

Nevada, "Everyone had servants," dinner "was always a great ceremony. . . . You wouldn't believe it with the little homes there in Carson."[12]

"Aiming for Better Communities"

Throughout the West, a great wave of Ladies Aid societies undertook fundraising and charity activities aimed at community improvement. Women founded libraries, donating books and volunteer hours to keep them open. Bazaars, box suppers, and socials raised money to help widows and orphans, provide scholarships for female students, and aid the poor. Groups like the Hebrew Ladies Benevolent Society assisted new Jewish settlers with loans and advice. Black pioneer women organized clubs, such as the Sojourner Truth Club of Los Angeles, the Black Woman's Beneficial Society, and the Sisters of Ethiopia, which served African American communities.

Women also aided starving families devastated by drought or grasshopper invasions. Male community leaders sometimes opposed this work, reluctant to call attention to such problems and discourage new settlers from coming. In one Kansas town, women refuted this logic in a letter to the local paper, offering to take the men to see the devastation firsthand. Wouldn't it hurt Kansas's image more, argued the women, to let settlers die of starvation? That said, they gathered food and clothing to aid the farmers.

Not surprisingly, women's reform efforts spilled into the political arena. The first issue uniting large numbers of women was the question of temperance—refusing to drink alcohol. Much of the West's violence—shootings, hangings, fighting, beatings, and abuse—stemmed from male drunkenness. In their role as protectors of family and society, women focused on alcohol's power to destroy. As early as the 1850s, some women demanded saloons close on Sundays. To this end, women's groups collected signatures and held public meetings.

In 1874, the Women's Christian Temperance Union (WCTU) formed in Ohio. By 1890, the WCTU was the largest women's organization in the United States. In 1878, Kansas alone had 26 local chapters. The organization proved a political training ground for women who learned how to petition, lobby, speak in public, and plan marches, rallies, and conventions. Kansan Carry Nation, whose first husband died of alcoholism, became the most famous temperance crusader in the country. Nation felt that fighting the "Demon Rum" was her God-given mission, and armed with a hatchet, she fearlessly invaded saloons, smashing bottles, mirrors, and furniture.

Most temperance supporters, however, used less violent means to highlight the issue. Women marched with banners blazoned with slogans like "Tremble King Alcohol, I shall grow up." Temperance workers lectured, wrote songs, lobbied state legislatures, passed out pamphlets, and sponsored essay contests in schools about the curses of alcohol. An 1889 publication appealed to Kansas Teachers, "The Schoolhouse Exalted, the Saloon Banished. Temperance, Health, and Moral Purity."[13] The work of temperance women eventually paved the way for the passage of the 18th Amendment, which—for a time—prohibited the manufacture and sale of alcoholic drinks throughout the United States.

"I Could, I Can, I Do"

Many women active in temperance work and other civic projects joined another growing movement—the fight for women's suffrage, the right to vote. Opponents argued that female suffrage would strip women of their femininity, destroy families, and even go against the laws of God. Many believed that as creatures of emotion, women lacked the education and reason to understand politics and voting.

Though the battle for women's rights originated in the East during the 1840s, the West garnered the first real gains. By 1861, Kansas women won the right to vote in school elections and hold property in their own names. An attempt in 1867 to grant women full suffrage in Kansas attracted national attention. Eastern suffrage heavy-hitters like Elizabeth Cady Stanton, Lucy Stone, and Susan B. Anthony traveled west to support the cause. Women lost the bitter battle, however, and Kansas women did not receive the vote in state and national elections until 1912. However, in 1887 they did gain the right to vote and run for office in city elections.

Wyoming women, on the other hand, quietly won the right to vote without rallies, petitions, or conventions. Perhaps influenced by his wife and 56-year-old Esther Morris, territorial senator William Bright introduced a bill in the Wyoming legislature in November 1869. The legislation grew partly from the belief that women needed the vote to effectively protect the family and society in such a rough and often lawless land. The bill proclaimed that every woman age 21 and older would have the right to vote and hold office. Before opposition could organize, the bill passed on December 10, and the governor signed it into law.

So, in Wyoming, on September 6, 1870, women turned out at the polls and exercised their legal right to vote. Elizabeth Cady Stanton later described Wyoming as "a blessed land, where for the first time in the history of the world, the true idea of a just government is realized, where woman is the political equal of man."[14]

Earlier that year, Esther Morris won appointment as a justice of the peace, and Wyoming became the first territory to select women for jury duty. Eastern newspapers ridiculed the idea, running a cartoon depicting women chomping cigars while nursing babies in the jury box. The caption read, "Baby, baby don't get in a fury, your mother's going to sit on a jury." But the judge in charge of the first trial with female jurors assured the women their right was protected by law, and "jeers and insults of a laughing crowd" would not drive them from their duty.[15]

In 1890, Wyoming entered the Union as the first state to include state and national voting rights for women in its constitution.

FRANK LESLIE'S ILLUSTRATED NEWSPAPER

NEW YORK—FOR THE WEEK ENDING NOVEMBER 24,

WOMAN SUFFRAGE IN WYOMING TERRITORY—SCENE AT THE POLLS IN CHEYENNE.

Wyoming women exercising their right to vote. *Library of Congress*

Other suffrage struggles ended in defeat. Utah women won the vote in 1870 and lost it in 1877. After losing their bid for suffrage in 1877, Colorado women won the vote in 1893, followed in 1896 by the women of Idaho and, again, Utah. By 1914, 11 of the last 18 states to join the Union—all of them in the West—had guaranteed women's suffrage, while none of the first 30 states allowed women to vote. Perhaps the difference lay in the West's newness. Writing new laws was easier than repealing long-standing ones. Susan B. Anthony wrote to a Utah newspaper in 1894:

> Now in the formative period of your constitution is the time to establish justice and equality to all the people. . . . Once ignored in your constitution—you'll be powerless to secure recognition as are we in the older states.[16]

Maybe Western men, who had to grant women the right to vote, appreciated the roles their wives, daughters, and mothers played in settling the West.

Perhaps another reason suffrage succeeded in the West was the support given to the movement by new grassroots political organizations: the Farmers' Alliance and the Populist Party. Both championed the rights of farmers and other working people and enjoyed a strong Western following in the 1880s and 1890s. Women flocked to the cause, seeking to preserve their homes and families, and for the first time, they played an important role in major political parties. They marched in processions, attended rallies, painted banners, and stood in wagon beds and on stages to address throngs of people.

Luna Kellie, who had first longed to vote on local school issues, blossomed into an active participant in the Farmers' Alliance. A mother of 11, she served as an editor, secretary, bookkeeper, and speaker for the Alliance. She also wrote several songs for Populist rallies and edited the Populist newspaper *Prairie Home* at her dining room table.

Annie Diggs of Kansas rose to leadership in the Alliance and the Populist organization. But the most famous voice of the Populist movement belonged to Mary Elizabeth Lease, a Kansan lawyer and mother of four. Lease held railroad companies and Wall Street bankers responsible for the farmer's financial troubles. "What the farmers need," she told her audience, "is to raise less corn and more hell!" Annie Diggs wrote of Lease, "A woman of other quality would have sunk under the avalanche. She was quite competent to cope with all that was visited upon her. Indeed, the abuse did her much service. The people but loved her the more for the enemies she made."[17]

A cartoon shows "A Chamber of Female Horrors" that included Carry Nation with her hatchet and Mary Lease with a rake. *Library of Congress*

Western newspapers noted women's involvement in politics and reported, "Women who never dreamed of becoming public speakers, grew eloquent in their zeal and fervor." Women, said another paper, "could talk straight to the point." And political humorist Joseph Billings summed things up: "Wimmin is everywhere."[18]

Western women reflected on their own accomplishments. As one mining town woman wrote her sister in Massachusetts, she had sent her roots into the barren Western soil and "gained unwanted strength in what seemed to you such unfavorable surroundings."[19]

Mary Elizabeth Lease

Political Firebrand

In the 1880s, on the prairies of Kansas, a woman stepped out of the shadows and onto the political platform. A tall, pale, dark-haired woman clad in a long black dress, her blue eyes flashing, she rose to speak on behalf of poor farmers and laborers. She mesmerized audiences, whether striding across a convention hall stage or standing in a wagon bed with rows of glossy corn stretching behind her. In a deep, rich voice that infused listeners with her passion, she harangued against greed and corruption and politicians who did nothing. Her name was Mary Lease. She set the plains on fire and gave voice to a political movement that ultimately failed but changed America along the way.

Born Mary Elizabeth Clyens in Pennsylvania on September 11, 1853, her parents were poor Irish immigrants. The death of her father and two brothers in the carnage of the Civil War

Mary Lease.
kansasmemory.org, Kansas State Historical Society

marked her early life. To Mary, they died fighting oppression and slavery, a continuation of her Irish ancestors' struggle against the English.

At age 17, in 1870, she boldly boarded a train bound for Kansas, answering the state's call for teachers and its promise of good pay. At a Catholic school in Osage Mission, Mary worked hard, sending money home to her mother. Like other young woman who headed west, Mary enjoyed a throng of male admirers. In January 1873, the 19-year-old wed a drugstore clerk named Charles Lease, a man past 30. She exchanged life as a teacher for life as a farmwife on the empty, wind-blown prairies of Kansas.

Charles borrowed money to pay the homesteader's land fees and buy tools, equipment, seeds, and animals. Like most farmers, the Leases began life mired deeply in debt. But farming held no guarantees, and during the 1870s and 1880s disaster after disaster ravaged the farms of the plains. In 1873, a great economic panic struck the country, shutting banks, textile mills, and coal mines. Grain merchants cancelled orders. By the end of the decade, harsh economic times escalated into violence, strikes, and riots. The government did nothing to ease the situation and often used force to end strikes or break up protests.

For farmers like Mary and Charles, even a good crop provided no relief. Prices for wheat and corn sank under the nation's money woes, and farmers' hopes to pay their own debts sank too. The next year brought further calamity—the 1874 invasion of grasshoppers. In a matter of hours, the greedy insects devoured crops, trees, and homes, leaving farmers with nothing to sell at all. With Mary pregnant and the family facing a bleak future, they moved to Denison, Texas, leaving their land for the loan company to repossess.

In Denison, Charles worked as a drugstore clerk. Mary gave birth to a son, whom they named after his father. The family stayed in Denison for a number of years and scraped by. Mary had two more babies, who died in infancy. Then in 1880 she had a daughter, Louise, and in 1883 another daughter, Grace, nicknamed Jimmie. Like many educated women on the frontier, Mary found the growing temperance movement an outlet for her energy.

But the promise of owning land still beckoned, and when the economy improved, the Leases moved back to Kansas. This second attempt at farming proved no better than the first; they lived in debt, always on the brink of ruin. Mary later looked back on those years and recalled, "I lived in the very midst of the desert, solitary, desolate, with no society save my children and no companions but our lonely thoughts. It was an awful life, dreary, monotonous, hard, bleak, and uninspiring."[20] Faced with failure again, the family moved to Wichita where Charles found work.

Railroads played a huge part in the farmers' plight. The government had handed railroad companies millions of acres of free land. The railroads campaigned for settlers and immigrants, promising land and prosperity. What they really offered was land so poor it could never grow a good crop—and they offered it at high prices. The railroad companies also controlled all transportation and charged farmers huge freight rates to ship their grain. They could charge high prices to store the grain as well, both before *and* after it shipped. Farmers' pleas to congressmen, senators, and governors to ease the prices charged by these monopolies fell on deaf ears. The railroad owners, with deep pockets for bribes and perks, controlled many politicians.

In Wichita, Mary put her education and her quick, argumentative mind to work. She trained to become a lawyer, "reading" law under the supervision of an established lawyer. At the same time, she gave birth to another son, named Ben Hur, raised and educated her children, cleaned house, and did the laundry, baking, cooking, and mending. She also washed clothes for her neighbors at 50 cents a day. She tacked legal papers onto the wall above her washtubs and studied while she worked.

Mary passed the Kansas bar examination and advertised in the *Wichita Eagle:* Would any women like to join forces for sharing education and good works? She gathered a little group, named the Hypatia Club after a female philosopher of ancient Greece, to discuss women's voting rights and other issues.

Mary's political philosophy quickly evolved through the prism of her own experiences. Had they failed at farming in part because of the greed of the railroads and loan companies? Had the good land been gobbled up by the railroads, leaving nothing for the poor farmer? Why did they have to pay a crushing interest rate on their loans? Congress had created the railroad beast. Congress had let a few get rich at the expense of millions of poor farmers and workers, and Mary blamed both political parties for failing the American people.

Mary made an impression. People described her dignity, her bearing, her shining eyes. She wore an air of distinction as finely as her tailored dresses. She commanded people with her presence, but what most captured people was Mary Lease's voice. One newspaperman later recalled, "The man or woman who did not halt in wonder at the sound of her voice had no music in his soul. . . . It was contralto, rich, even mellow, of a quality beyond that possessed by any of the great actresses of my knowledge."[21] Mary's speech could ring with humor or scorn, and people took notice of what she said. In honor of Saint Patrick's Day in March 1886, she made her first public lecture, an audience-pleasing appeal for Irish liberty, sprinkled with Irish poetry and harsh words for British imperialism.

Mary immersed herself more and more in local affairs. She promoted school hygiene, the vote for women, and farmers' issues. As she warmed to her political causes, she spared no one from her sharp tongue. She irked some people by the mere fact that she called herself Mary Lease, instead of Mrs. Charles Lease, as they felt a well-bred lady should do. But she got results. The Kansas State Legislature became the first in the country to grant women the right to vote in city and town elections.

The 1880s submerged many farmers and laborers in further misery. Low wages left little for emergencies; people needed small loans just to pay off doctor's bills. Harsh winters killed cattle and sheep, and blazing dry summers withered crops in the fields. Defeated, many abandoned their farms, hoping to escape starvation. The Leases, a family of six, struggled too, though Charles at least earned a wage to feed his family. Mary took in boarders to help pay the mortgage. By 1888, an election year, bitterness swept over much of the country. Why did politicians do nothing to ease the suffering of the very people who had elected them to office?

Men mostly ignored the political efforts of Mary and her Hypatia group, but Mary had turned a corner. Women might lack the vote, but they could write, they could speak, they could organize, and they could be heard. For Mary, winning the vote became only a piece of the puzzle in the quest for human rights. She prepared to turn her back on the Democrats and Republicans who had failed the working poor, and support a new political party—one filled with radical ideas to sweep change into American government.

The Knights of Labor, the first general labor organization, admitted women to membership, and Mary Lease joined. But the Knights of Labor shunned political involvement, while Mary believed political change created social change. She also joined the Union Labor Party, which supported government ownership of the railroads, government irrigation programs for farmers, and laws against child labor.

Mary Lease made her first political speech to the Wichita Union Labor Party and discovered her rare talent to "put my whole soul in my speech." The first applause hooked Mary, and she became determined to use her speaking in "the cause of right." Her speeches mingled wit and sarcasm with bits of Shakespeare and Emerson, enthralling her listeners.

The Union Labor Party pushed Mary to the forefront as they planned their platform for the 1888 elections. They called for votes for women, an income tax that taxed the rich more than the poor, and the direct election by the people of US senators. Across Kansas, Mary spoke against the Republican government that controlled the state, the loan companies that charged high interest rates, and the railroad monopolies. She also successfully navigated the Knights of Labor into the political arena. Mary differed from many women, even those seeking the vote—she wanted to have a say in politics, say who could run for office, and maybe even run for office herself.

When longtime Kansas senator John Ingalls brushed Mary aside—"Women have no place in politics," he said—she took those as fighting words. And though the Union Labor Party showed poorly in the election, Mary Lease had ignited a spark in Kansas. The party opened a reform newspaper, the *Independent*, to kindle the fire, with Mary at the helm. "In sending out to the world a journal devoted to reform, truth, and justice, I am fully aware of the responsibility I have assumed and the unpopularity of the task I have undertaken. While I expect ridicule and criticism," she assured readers, "I do not fear either."[22]

Across the Western prairies and a few Southern states like Georgia, reformers and radicals joined with the Farmers' Alliance movement to form a new political entity called the People's Party. Soon known as the Populists, they pledged to run candidates for state offices in the 1890 elections.

One rallying point was that banks borrowed money at 2 percent interest but turned around and charged farmers as much as 11 percent interest on loans. Populists wanted farmers to have direct, low-interest loans from the government. They also wanted an end to the railroads' monopoly to set exorbitant prices for grain storage and freight charges.

The harvest of 1889 yielded a perfect crop of Kansas corn, but farmers could only sell their corn for 10 cents a bushel—less than it had cost to raise it. In Chicago, corn sold for 50 cents a bushel, with the profits going to the railroads and grain merchants. Meanwhile, the city's poor could not afford grain. Politicians blamed and insulted farmers. "What is needed," said Senator Ingalls, "is some legislation that will give brains to the brainless, thrift to the thriftless, industry [work] to the irresolute, and discernment to the fools."[23]

Mary Lease traveled like a whirlwind across Kansas that summer of 1890, delivering 160 speeches urging people to action. "When I get through with the silk-hatted easterners they will know that the Kansas prairies are on fire!" she thundered.[24]

Thousands flocked to hear her message, and when she raised her arms and exhorted the crowds to raise less corn and more hell, people cheered.

"Wall Street owns the country," she informed her audience. "It is no longer a government of the people, by the people, and for the people, but a government of Wall Street, by Wall Street, and for Wall Street. The great common people of this country are slaves, and monopoly is the master. . . . The [political] parties lie to us and the political speakers mislead us."

The farmers and the farmers' wives loved Mary. "We were told two years ago to go to work and raise a big crop, that was all we needed," she cried. "We went to work and plowed and planted; the rains fell, the sun shone, nature smiled, and we raised the big crop that they told us to; and what came of it? Eight-cent corn, ten-cent oats, two-cent beef and no price at all for butter and eggs—that's what came of it."

"The politicians said we suffered from overproduction. Overproduction," she asked, "when 10,000 little children, so statistics tell us, starve to death every year in the United States, and over 100,000 shopgirls in New York are forced to sell their virtue for the bread their niggardly wages deny them."

Mary listed the peoples' demands: "We want money, land, and transportation. We want the abolition of the National Banks, and we want the power to make loans direct from the government. We want the foreclosure system wiped out. . . . We will stand by our homes," she urged them, "and stay by our fireside by force if necessary, and we will not pay our debts to the loan-shark companies until the government pays its debts to us. The people are at bay." She warned, "Let the bloodhounds of money who dogged us thus far beware."[25]

As the elections neared, party newspapers attacked Mary, branding her as "a miserable caricature of womanhood, hideously ugly in features and foul of tongue." "In a month the . . . goggle-eyed nightmare will be out of a job," predicted one paper.[26] They changed her middle name to Ellen, which rhymed with "yellin,'" and eventually they attacked her through her children.

On November 4, the nation voted, and the next day Republicans and Democrats took note. For the first time, a third party, the Populists, had gained governors and control of state legislatures, including that of Kansas, and Populist congressmen were headed to Washington. Longtime Kansas senator John Ingalls, who'd scorned Mary's political efforts, lost his seat. A Republican newspaper lamented on the disaster, "As usual, there was a woman in the case . . . Mrs. Lease."[27] The Populists looked ahead to the presidential election of 1892 with rising hope.

Mary did her part to swell the Populists' momentum. She visited Georgia, a populist stronghold, and plainly declared people could call her whatever they wished—an anarchist, a socialist, a communist. "I hold to the theory that if one man has not enough to eat three times a day and another man has $25,000,000, that last man has something that belongs to the first."[28] To the WCTU, she pleaded for "no more millionaires, and no more paupers, . . . and no more little waifs of humanity starving for a crust of bread. No more gaunt-faced, hollow-eyed girls in factories, and no more little boys reared in poverty and crime for the penitentiaries and the gallows."[29] She also spoke before the National Council of Women, championing the cause of female suffrage.

In July 1892, Mary attended the Populist Party convention in Omaha. She helped shape the party platform which supported the right of workers to form unions and called for government ownership of the railroads, telephones, and telegraphs. Populists demanded money reform and the right of the people to borrow directly from the government at low rates. They wanted a graduated income tax, return to the government of railroad land not used by the railroads, an eight-hour workday for industry, direct election of US senators by the voters, and the right of voters to propose laws and vote on laws through referendums. One plank was missing from the platform, however—voting rights for women. Mary went along with this for the sake of party unity; others feared this controversial plank might cost the Populists votes in the election. Mary made the speech seconding the motion to nominate General James Weaver as the Populist candidate for president.

Again, Mary Lease stood as a prominent voice for the Populist movement. She campaigned tirelessly, urging farmers and laborers to band together against big business and mainstream politicians. She swept across the Western states, speaking to crowds numbering in the thousands. Noted candidate Weaver, "She is an orator of marvelous power. . . . Her hold upon the laboring people was something wonderful. They almost worshipped her from one end of the country to the other."[30]

Mary Lease headed into the heart of the South to states like Georgia, Virginia, and Tennessee, where she hoped to sever the ties binding white voters to the Democratic Party. But here, whipped up by Democratic papers, the crowds heckled and threatened the Populist speakers. People pelted Mary with eggs. Southern papers attacked General Weaver, who'd served in the Union army, as a war criminal.

Fearing a loss of power, Southern Democrats even threatened to lynch the Populists. A Tennessee paper made the case: "John Brown came from Kansas to the South to assassinate all slaveholders. Now, Mrs. Lease comes South, from the same state, with the declaration that the Negro should be made the equal of the white man, and that all difference between the sexes should be obliterated. Great God! What next from Kansas?"[31]

Though many populist candidates failed in the November 1892 elections, Kansas, thanks in part to Mary's efforts, voted Populist for president. But Populists in the South and East went down in defeat, hurt by intimidation and the fact that factory workers did not band together with farmers.

Many people hoped the Kansas legislature would appoint Mary to take the vacant seat of Senator Preston Plumb. Letters poured in supporting Mary's appointment as the first female senator. But if the Populists hoped to pass any of their reforms, they needed to join with Democrats to gain a majority over Republicans. Mary hadn't spared Democrats in her speeches, and the party retaliated by forcing through a Democratic judge to fill the Senate seat.

Mary felt restless, not sure about this new marriage with the Democrats. She feared the Populists would lose their hard edge, giving up reform for the sake of keeping themselves in office. For Mary Lease, this was no time to keep silent. Both 1893 and 1894 brought further economic disaster to the country. Armed troops clashed with striking railroad workers in Chicago. Factories closed. Homeless and jobless people wandered the land.

In Boston, Mary galvanized a throng of unemployed people, reminding them, "What we want is justice for all and special privileges for none. . . . Instead of bankers and lawyers for legislators get your representatives from the laboring classes. . . . It is the duty of the government you defend in war to feed you in time of peace."[32] In midterm elections, angry people again turned their backs on Republicans and Democrats and voted Populist in state and local elections. Would the presidential election of 1896 finally see a people's movement?

Instead, the Democrats determined to pick off Populist voters by adopting some Populist planks. This included the cry for "free silver," a plan to coin or print supplies of money backed by silver rather than gold. They hoped "cheap money" would mean more cash in the pockets of the poor. Democrats used their free-silver platform to lure Populist voters to the party. The Populist Party splintered—should they fuse with the Democrats or stand on their own?

Mary stood for going it alone, much to the disbelief of many Populist leaders. At the national convention, just as Mary prepared to speak, the lights went out; the hall's darkness swallowed her voice. The party she had helped found and promote with every fiber of her being had turned out the lights and decided to merge with the Democrats. Meanwhile, the Democrats abandoned much of the Populist platform except for the free-silver movement. Mary followed through campaigning for Democratic candidate William Jennings Bryan, but the Democrats lost the election. The Populist Party had been broken.

A political creature, Mary spent the years after 1896 working as a journalist and lecturer, keeping her causes alive and a small income flowing. She left Kansas for New York, and she left her husband. With son Charley handling her bookings, she toured the nation, and people turned out in droves to hear her. Joseph Pulitzer hired her to write about politics for the *New York World*. She pulled no punches, clearly still angry at the Democrats who'd swallowed the Populist Party whole.

Mary remained a fighting radical until the end of her days. She offered poor clients free legal advice. She drummed home the Populist message and spoke about peace, birth control, and women's rights. She penned magazine articles. She put all four of her children through college. She supported politicians seeking change: Eugene Debs for the Socialist Party, Theodore Roosevelt in his third party run with the Progressive Party, and Democratic reformer Woodrow Wilson.

Before her death in October 1933, Mary Lease saw many of the causes she'd fought to win for 25 years come to pass, including government regulation of the railroads. The graduated income tax became law in 1913, as well as the direct election of US senators. In 1920 the 19th Amendment granted women the right to vote. Mary Lease must have felt satisfaction, if not vindication. As she'd once said, "My work was not in vain. . . . The seeds we sowed out in Kansas did not fall on barren ground."[33]

Carry Nation

"Hatchetation" Against the Devil's Brew

People, especially Easterners, easily turned Carry Nation into a caricature. Past the age of 50 (an age when "proper" females melted away into the wallpaper), Carry stood out. She crusaded in unfashionable dress while berating women for wearing dead birds on their hats, she preached, and she snatched cigarettes from the lips of surprised males. But what really panicked people about Carry Nation—especially saloon keepers—was the hatchet gleaming in her hands and the fearless glint in her eyes.

"God has his crowd and the Devil has his," she wrote, "and every man and woman is in one or the other."[34] Deeply religious, Nation believed God had chosen her path for her. She needed to fight for the downtrodden. If that meant rescuing prostitutes, preaching temperance, giving away her earnings, smashing saloons, and facing jail, the Kansan grandmother was up for the task.

Born in Kentucky in 1846, Carry's family moved to Missouri, to Texas, and back to Missouri, in the turbulent years before and

Antialcohol crusader Carry Nation. *Library of Congress*

during the Civil War. At age 19, she fell in love with Charles Gloyd, a boarder at her parent's home. Gloyd had been a captain in the Union army, studied medicine, and taught school. Her parents disapproved of Gloyd's drinking, however, and forbid Carry to speak with him. But Carry craved affection and failed to resist the handsome man who read Shakespeare to her and spoke of his admiration and love for her. They exchanged secret letters, passed between them in a book.

The circumstances left Carry torn between duty to her parents and love for Charles. Finally, with "heart burnings and scalding tears," she implored him to establish himself and prove to her parents he could support a family. Gloyd moved away, and the courtship continued via letters for the next two years. Carry's mother did her best to drive her daughter from the relationship, but the couple wed in November 1867.

Troubles burdened the marriage almost immediately. Gloyd turned distant or stayed out late, leaving his bride "hungry for his caresses and love."[35] The drinking problem she'd ignored during courtship robbed them of happiness. Her husband staggered home drunk and shut himself away. Gloyd drank too much to work and spent what money they had on liquor.

Six months into the marriage, knowing she was pregnant, Carry returned to her parents' home. "I do love my mother and father so much," she wrote Charles, "but there is no one half so dear as my husband."[36] Her mother threatened to turn her out if she continued writing Gloyd. In September 1868, Carry gave birth to her daughter, Charlien. Her parents forbid her to tell Gloyd the child had been born.

She saw Charles once more, her mother's threat ringing in her ears: she could never return home again if she decided to stay with her husband. Gloyd died on March 20, 1869, a young man riddled by alcohol. Carry would always regret leaving him, and she kept his romantic letters for the rest of her life. At age 22, she faced widowhood with a baby and no money.

She felt anger at herself and her parents, and the months ahead filled her with doubts and remorse and worries. She isolated herself, felt lonely, and questioned whether God loved her and would help her. Years later, she viewed these dark years as a test that created her future role as activist. "Had I married a man I could have loved, God never could have used me. . . . The very thing (a happy marriage) I was denied caused me to have a desire to secure it for others."[37]

Carry moved in with Charles's mother and eventually earned a teacher's certificate to support herself. But she lost her job after losing her temper with the district superintendent, and she vowed in her diary to control her thoughts and make no harsh retorts. The path to happiness, she decided, lay in conforming and keeping to a woman's role in life. In December 1874, she did what many widows did to secure their future—she married a widower named David Nation, a man of 47 with five children, in need of a wife and homemaker.

David Nation worked as a lawyer, farmer, and minister, sometimes with little success. The family moved to Texas. At one point, David abandoned Carry to deal alone with their failing farm. The heavy workload on top of financial worries left her ill. Money soon caused a rift in the marriage, and Carry again felt she could not secure her husband's love. But she created a place for herself, starting two successful boardinghouses, which provided income as well as a sense of independence.

Religion became her comfort, especially when Charlien developed a jaw disease in 1880 that would eventually cause her to lose her teeth and destroy her health. Carry borrowed money to take her daughter for treatments. Fearing Charlien would never marry, Carry hustled the 20-year-old into marriage with Alex McNabb, a reaction that haunted Carry in years to come. She wondered if the seed of Charlien's poor health sprang from her father's drunkenness.

In 1884, Carry Nation experienced a "baptism of the Holy Ghost," a spiritual awakening. She began having visions where God laid out the path she should follow. She embraced the emotional side of religion, shouting, clapping, and falling to her knees. Instead of loyalty to one church, she saw the whole world as the mission for her good works. She preached, she corrected—and in a time when males dominated church leadership—Carry seemed a threatening figure to the status quo. She never apologized for her religious fervor, taming critics this way: "I like to go just as far as the farthest. I like my religion like my oysters and beefsteak—piping hot!"[38]

In 1890, David and Carry moved to Kansas; the state was a hotbed of activism—Populist politics, woman's suffrage, and temperance issues that attracted Carry. After six years they moved again, this time to Oklahoma. Here Carry trained as an osteopathic healer and continued her organizations to help the needy. But she could not help her daughter when Charlien arrived to visit in 1897 with her own children. Her daughter's unhappiness in her marriage, her health broken by the jaw disease and repeated pregnancies, left Carry at a loss.

Back in Kansas in 1899, Carry joined the antialcohol crusade, which politicized more women than any other issue. When men drank, women and children suffered physical abuse and loss of home and security. A wife's wages belonged to her husband; he could drink them away, and she had no right to protect her family's finances. Saloons offered male-only retreats; a man abandoned his wife to go drink and maybe even to cavort with prostitutes who also inhabited saloons. Women feared not only for their health and homes, they feared also for their children, who might be lured into bars to smoke and drink.

The Women's Christian Temperance Union (WCTU), founded in Ohio in 1874 and then established across the country, served as a political training ground for thousands of women. The group's methods involved praying and singing outside bars and saloons, what Carry called "moral suasion." In 1881, Kansas banned the sale and manufacture of alcohol, but barkeepers paid off politicians and police who ignored the law and protected the saloons. Without the right to vote, women had little real power to change laws or kick out corrupt elected officials.

Within a year of returning to Kansas, Carry Nation, who'd lost her first husband and home to alcohol, undertook a stronger approach than singing and praying. Her method required smashing. In a quote from the *Kansas City Star* in January 1901, she defended her violent methods: "Moral suasion! If there's anything that's weak and worse than useless it's this moral suasion. . . . These hell traps of Kansas have fattened for twenty years on moral suasion. The saloon man loves moral suasion. . . . If a snake came into your house to kill your boy you would not use moral suasion you would look for a poker!"[39]

Carry Nation was not the first to smash barrels of whiskey, but she soon became a symbol of the radical prohibition movement. She took the first plunge in June 1900 at Kiowa, Kansas, following God's orders to smash up the "joints." She entered several saloons that day, using bricks to smash anything that would shatter and then delivering a sermon to surprised gawkers. The mayor, sheriff, and town attorney debated what to do—and then let her go. The news of her raid spread quickly. Newspapers just as quickly labeled her an old lady "of unsound mind," who should be "kept at home by her people."[40]

But Mrs. Nation did not stay home. In late December, she boarded a train for Wichita, where she destroyed property at several establishments, most notably smashing up the elegant Carey Hotel bar to the tune of $3,000 worth of damage, shattering mirrors, bottles, and crystal glasses, and destroying a large nude painting, "Cleopatra at the Bath." This time police threw Carry in jail, where officers quarantined her in the basement to keep her quiet, leaving her to lie on the floor. She viewed it all as a tribulation to overcome and remained confident that God would deliver her from her troubles.

Released after nine days in jail, an unrepentant Nation returned to smashing, this time with a small group of like-minded women. On January 21, 1901, armed for the first time with a hatchet, she led her followers on a smashing expedition through Wichita. Thousands gathered in the streets for the entertainment value. One saloon worker shoved a gun against her head, and a policeman knocked her down. All the women were hauled off to jail but were released after promising no more joint smashing in Wichita for 24 hours.

Carry left immediately for Enterprise, Kansas, where she delivered a temperance talk and led a crowd to a nearby saloon where she demolished the interior and broke windows. The saloon owner hired prostitutes to beat and whip Carry; she left town bruised and battered. A month later, she stormed the Kansas legislature and scolded the members, ending with, "A good solid vote is the best thing in the world with which to smash the saloons. You wouldn't give me the vote, so I had to use a rock!"[41]

Her constant travel and devotion to her cause strained Carry's already unhappy marriage. In 1901, David Nation filed for divorce, charging that Carry was "unmindful of her duties as a housewife," had grown bossy, and subjected him to "gross neglect."[42] The scandalous divorce hurt a woman who saw herself as trying to save American families. But Carry's embarrassment proved good fun for her detractors, including Thomas Edison, who made a film titled *Why Mr. Nation Wants a Divorce.* In the silent movie, Mr. Nation feebly attempts to care for several children, before giving up and crawling into bed with a bottle of whiskey. Mrs. Nation, portrayed by a robust actor in a black dress, barges into the room, snatches the bottle from her husband's lips, beats him, and then spanks him.

Carry's actions sparked saloon smashings across the country and as far away as France. From 1901 on, Carry Nation lived in a whirlwind of celebrity and travel. She continued smashing illegal saloons in Kansas—calling her assaults "hatchetations"—and sometimes leading an army of several thousand through the streets. As one supporter noted, "It's a wonder there are not millions of Mrs. Nations in the world, after the suffering which women have endured from husbands or sons who are drunkards. . . . She is in the right . . . enforcing the law."[43]

In states without prohibition laws, she shoved her way in to shake hands and preach to the sinners. She did not shy away from invading the worst sort of joints, filled with drunkards and prostitutes. "If Jesus ate with publicans and sinners I can talk to them," she wrote.[44] She played off her name, Carry Amelia Nation, for she would "carry a nation" from its abuse of alcohol and nicotine.

She was a sensation, an oddity, a prophet for change, and even people who decried her violent methods and thought her a lunatic wanted a piece of her notoriety. She attracted crowds and sold newspapers. And if Carry wasn't interesting enough just as she was, papers fabricated tidbits about her, even claiming she wielded her hatchet as a six-foot Amazon would and required extra-large policemen to wrestle her to the ground.

Nation traveled into hostile territory when she took on big cities like Chicago, Los Angeles, and New York, where one letter writer assured her "there are a good many saloon keepers here itching for your coming . . . awaiting you with a great big club."[45] The merciless Eastern press dubbed her ugly, savage, revolting, unsexed or sexually perverted, manly, and "wild and westernly." She was dangerous, a woman outside her place. Many journalists branded her insane. Nation took it all in stride. "They tell me I am unlady-like; that I'm out of my sphere, or ought to work in a different way. But when I'm doing God's work I don't go to the devil for methods!" she told the *Topeka Daily Capital*.[46]

Clearly Carry Nation was different from the refined wives who worked for causes in the East. She wasn't pale and tightly laced in a corset; she was stout, tanned, and plainly dressed. Her free use of "hell" and "damnation" in her lectures shocked Eastern sensibilities, but she treated everyone as equals and talked to people like a mother would. She was witty, funny, if a bit rough, and her plain speech usually brought people around to at least listen. She'd proved too radical for the WCTU, though, which distanced itself from Carry's smashing, claiming Mrs. Nation "has a method all her own, and one which is not found in the plan or the work of WCTU."[47]

Between 1901 and 1909, police carted Carry off to jail more than 30 times, and she was hauled before judges and fined for destruction of property and inciting riots. During one smashing spree, she was arrested and let go four times in one day. To help pay her court fines, Carry sold little pewter hatchet pins and water bottles; most of her other earnings went to charity. She also published and sold subscriptions to two newspapers, the *Smasher's Mail* and the *Hatchet*. In 1904, she self-published an autobiography explaining her life and actions: *The Use and Need of the Life of Carry A. Nation*.

She appeared anywhere she could to reach her audience, performing onstage in a Broadway play, lecturing in vaudeville and burlesque houses, and spending the summer months on the Chautauqua touring circuit. "I am fishing," she wrote. "I go where the fish are . . . I found the theatres stocked with the boys of our country. They are not found in churches."[48]

In 1905, Carry moved to Oklahoma where she successfully worked to put prohibition into the new state constitution. She next moved to Washington, DC, agitating for a national prohibition law. In 1908, her fame carried her to Scotland and England, where she was touted as the American Saloon Smasher. At age 63 in December 1909, Carry Nation carried out her last joint smashing at Union Station in Washington, DC. Exhausted from all her work and travels, she finally settled down in Arkansas. She purchased a home in Eureka Springs, christened it Hatchet Hall, and turned it into a safe haven for the wives of alcoholics. Carry herself often cooked the meals there. She also established a school and a home to assist the elderly.

Carry continued her summer speaking tours but now spent more time with her family. Charlien, her health drastically deteriorated, arrived from Texas with her children and lived under Carry's care. In 1910, Carry fought to prevent Charlien's husband, who had physically abused his wife, from committing her daughter to an insane asylum—a battle Carry lost. It broke Carry's heart and robbed her of hope; her niece noted this last act "was more than she could live with."[49] Carry Nation died June 9, 1911, of heart failure.

Carry Nation galvanized thousands of women and men to activism in the temperance movement. She also fought for women's rights and against tobacco and never turned away from helping those in need. Her headstone bears the epitaph she wished: SHE HATH DONE WHAT SHE COULD. More to the point, however, may be the way she sometimes signed her name: "Carry Nation, widow and prophet of God, friend of mankind and enemy of alcohol," written boldly across the paper.

6
CLASH OF CULTURES

"My People talked fearfully that winter about those they called our white brothers."

—Sarah Winnemucca

Where white pioneer women often saw an unforgiving wilderness, Native American women saw a loved and familiar home. From the Great Plains and Rocky Mountains to the Southwestern desert and the forests of the Pacific Northwest, Native American women lived very differently from the white newcomers. But they also lived differently from one another—with different languages, beliefs, homes, clothing, and food.

Though Indian men hunted and fished for food and protected their tribes from enemies, a village's well-being depended heavily on women's work. As with white women, Indian women's lives chiefly revolved around home and children, food, clothing, and shelter. Life was difficult and food sometimes scarce, especially in winter or for tribes living in desert areas. Generosity with food, a symbol of welcome and nurturing, earned a woman respect, and in many Indian societies, women held the keys to food distribution.

A woman's knowledge of edible plants helped her gather fruits, nuts, seeds, roots, bulbs, and herbs. In farming tribes, women tended and harvested crops and preserved food for winter. Among the Hopi and Zuni people of the Southwest, women owned the fields, and men often worked them. At harvest time, women took charge, drying and grinding vast amounts of corn into meal. Kneeling before the grinding stone for hours at a

This Edward Curtis photo shows Hopi women grinding corn.
legendsofamerica.com

time, women murmured prayers and songs of thanks for the good harvest. A woman considered grinding 25 pounds of cornmeal a good day's work and shared her bounty with relatives who had no daughters to help them.

After a buffalo hunt, a Plains woman joined in a day of feasting and listening to stories of the hunters' bravery. She faced hours of hard and bloody work as she butchered the 1,500-pound animals, cutting the meat into long, thin spirals to hang over drying racks. Sun and the plains wind dried and blackened the strips into jerky. Then it would be ready to store or grind into pemmican, a protein-rich mixture of dried meat, berries, and fat.

An Apsaroke (Crow) woman works on a buffalo hide in this Edward Curtis photo. *Library of Congress*

Outside the camp lay rafts of buffalo skins, the raw hides stretched and pegged to the ground. Women scraped away the fat and tissue, applying chemicals extracted from the animal's brain, liver, and fat, and slowly working the skin into a soft usable material. Some hides, left to harden, were turned into storage cases called parfleches. Sinews became thread; bones became needles and tools. Indian women wasted nothing of the great animal, thousands of pounds of meat, skin, organs, and bone, all used and appreciated as a gift from the Creator.

Plains women sewed their homes from buffalo skins; a large teepee needed about 22 hides. Like white settlers, Indian women often called on one another for assistance in building their homes, preparing a feast for those who helped. The finished teepee, and all the furnishings and equipment inside, belonged to the woman. Whenever the tribe moved, she took down, packed, unpacked, and set up her family's teepee at the new location. Women in other regions also built the family home: the Navajo hogan, the Apache wickiup, and the mud bricks and adobe apartments of the Pueblo people.

Women made their families' clothing from animal skins and furs or materials woven from wool, softened bark, and grasses. Leather moccasins or sandals protected their feet. Tribes living in northern climates added leggings, blankets, and buffalo-skin robes for winter.

Many Indian women owned not only the property they brought into their marriages but anything they made afterward as well: tools, utensils, bags, and storage containers. Indian women did not waste time making decorative items that served no useful purpose; instead, their talents and creativity lent beauty to everyday objects. Some tribes esteemed a woman's skill in decorative arts like a warrior's deeds in battle.

Southwestern peoples like the Paiute, Navajo, Pima, Papago, and Apache excelled at creating tightly woven baskets. Tribes of the Pacific Northwest and the Navajo to the south became expert weavers of fabric. Navajo weaving was said to originate with Spider Woman, a legendary figure who long ago taught her art to the people. Because women owned and tended the Navajo sheep and goat herds, they wielded economic power many other Indian women (and white women) lacked.

The Pueblo women of the Southwest crafted beautiful pottery. One Zuni woman claimed she painted all her thoughts onto her pottery. Nomadic Plains tribes needed more durable items

An Achomawi woman of northeastern California works on a basket in this Edward Curtis photo. *Library of Congress*

than pottery. Plains women used buffalo hides to make everything from storage bags to cradleboards, clothing, and moccasins, and they decorated items with paint, beads, and dyed porcupine quills in an array of colors and designs. The all-important beads were formed from bone, shell, animal teeth, nuts, seeds, and stones, and later women used colored glass beads received from white traders. Skilled Cheyenne women belonged to an exclusive quilling society that passed on the art to younger women.

Like white pioneer women, Indian women enjoyed socializing and recreation. Dances celebrated successful harvests, hunts, and battles, provided courting opportunities for young couples, and played a part in religious ceremonies. Where white society thought physical strength diminished a woman's femininity, the strongest, healthiest Indian women earned respect as good workers and mothers. Indian women swam, raced horses, and sledded in winter. Cheyenne women played a kind of football. Pima and Papago women loved field hockey, a game played with balls that were fashioned from hide and stuffed with grass or animal hair. Quieter pastimes included string games, like cat's cradle, and gambling games played using bone dice.

For people who lived closely with nature, the mysteries of life and death lay everywhere to be seen, and were woven into the very fabric of an Indian woman's life—in the seasons, the hunt, the planting, and the harvest. Prayers asked for food and good health for the tribe. In some tribes, women, as well as men, hoped for a vision or spiritual dream to show them the road to a good life. Many native cultures revered female spirits like White Buffalo Calf Woman, who brought the sacred pipe to the Lakota and taught them to live as one with all creatures, the earth, and the sky.

In many tribes, women gained power and honor with age. Passing on the wisdom of a lifetime, they offered advice about tribal matters, history, religion, and medicine. Children listened with respect while elders taught the ways and stories of their people. Some tribes had female chiefs, mature women distinguished through their generosity and hard work.

Indian women gained status through other roles as well. A medicine woman earned both respect and status as a healer, plying her tools of special songs, prayers, and treatments made from mosses, roots, barks, and leaves. Tribes expected and admired bravery from women as well as men. Women followed men to war as cooks and nurses. A Comanche woman possessed horse skills equal to those of a warrior and could defend her village if necessary, as did Yellow-Haired Woman of the Cheyenne, or Lozen of the Apache. The Blackfeet called a strong-minded woman "manly hearted."

"We Eyed Them with a Good Deal of Curiosity"

Indian women viewed the white people invading their lands with both fear and curiosity. Indian mothers thought the strangers might steal or murder their children. The pale-skinned females wore ridiculous clothes—what shapes actually lurked beneath those hoop skirts and bustles? Physical punishment of Indian children was almost completely unknown, yet native women saw white parents spank and beat their offspring. White peoples' sense of individual self-interest seemed foreign to tribal communal societies. Native Americans especially could not understand the white settlers' desire to possess land and change it to suit their needs.

White women heading west in the 1840s also felt fear and curiosity. Luzena Wilson hid her children whenever their party encountered Native Americans. She'd heard plenty about "their bloody deeds, the massacre of harmless white men, torturing helpless women, carrying away captive innocent babes."[1] First meetings were usually friendly, although some women voiced derision at the Indians' appearance—"painted, dirty, nauseous-smelling savages," wrote one.[2] Descriptions of Native Americans as "treacherous," "thieving," and "bloodthirsty" appeared in white women's journals. Emigrant women did not understand that in most Indian societies visitors exchanged gifts. Instead, when Indians expected food or gifts from the newcomers, white women condemned them for begging.

Their journals noted, however, that Indians could be of use: "I traded an apron today for a pair of moccasins of the Indians." "We have engaged our passage down the Columbia this morning in a canoe with the Indians."[3] "Have also a good many Indians and bought fish of them. They all seem peaceful and friendly."[4] One woman advised new settlers to pack a supply of calico shirts to trade.

But often alone on their homesteads, white women feared the sudden appearance of curious Indians at their cabin doors. "These Osage are said to be friendly," wrote Miriam Colt, "but I cannot look at their painted visages without a shudder."[5] She clutched her children to her side, afraid the Indians would steal them. If provoked, a white woman defended her home and family, though her weapon might be nothing more than a broom. Unwelcome Indian visitors usually retreated. For the most part, when fear died down, white women viewed Indians as people to be pitied—inferior, they believed, to the white race.

White women journeying west heard horrific tales of the rape and torture of females captured by Indians. George Custer ordered that, in case of attack, any man near Elizabeth was to shoot her instead of letting her fall into Indian hands. Olive Oatman, Rachel Plummer, Matilda Lockhart, and others survived abusive captivities and bore the scars and mutilations from the ordeals for the rest of their lives.

"The White People Have Taken"

As the trickle of white pioneers turned into a flood of hundreds of thousands, violence escalated between Indians and whites. Native Americans watched helplessly as diseases carried by settlers raced through their villages, killing hundreds. They saw the buffalo and other food sources destroyed. White hunters with rifles killed hundreds of the huge shaggy creatures in a single day, leaving carcasses to rot and pushing the animals to near extinction.

Blue-coated army troops struck Indian villages, killing women, children, and old people as they fled. Soldiers hunted down ragged bands of Indians, driving tribes to surrender to life on reservations. Indian women knew the wrenching pain of loss, the loss of everything. An Omaha woman

A Navajo woman and her baby, 1860s. *Library of Congress*

wondered "if there is anything in [white] civilization which will make good to us what we have lost."[6]

Tribe by tribe, band by band, the government forced Indian peoples onto reservation lands, lands often located hundreds of miles from beloved homelands where tribes had lived since before memory. Proud cultures suffered. The US government whisked Indian children away to boarding schools, forced them to learn English and wear the clothing of white America, and stripped them of their own languages and customs. Government Indian agencies banned hunting, dances, ceremonies, and religious practices. For men considered brave hunters and warriors, reservation life proved empty and meaningless.

Overall, however, the rhythm of life did not change as sharply for Indian women as it did for men. Children still needed to be raised; food had to be cooked, clothes sewn, and homes kept. Often Indian women managed to preserve their tribal heritage. "A nation is not conquered," went a Plains Indian saying, "until the hearts of its women are on the ground. Then it is finished, no matter how brave its warriors or how strong their weapons."[7]

The early reservation years proved especially difficult for people used to freedom and food enough to feed themselves. Corruption polluted the government reservation system. Agents sold off food and clothing meant for the Indians and allowed whites to squat on the best reservation lands. For thousands of Indian people, reservation life brought starvation and mistreatment.

During the late 1870s and 1880s, several Indian women, including a Paiute named Sarah Winnemucca and an Omaha named Susette La Flesche, gained national prominence fighting the injustice shown their people. Both women spoke English, and La Flesche had been educated in the East. Seen as exotic by white audiences, they lectured in Eastern cities, wrote, and traveled to Washington, DC, to speak on behalf of Native Americans. Sarah Winnemucca pleaded for an end to the terrible treatment of reservation Indians, especially her own people. "The women," she wrote of Paiute society, "know as much as the men do, and their advice is often asked." She chastised white legislators by writing, "If women could go into your Congress, I think justice would soon be done to the Indians."[8] Wrote La Flesche, "It's all a farce when you say you are trying to civilize us, then, after we educate ourselves, refuse us positions of responsibility and leave us utterly powerless to help ourselves."[9]

Finding Common Ground

Most white settlers never tried to understand the native people whose lands they stole and whose lives they destroyed. But a few army wives voiced sympathy for the Native Americans they also viewed as "hostiles." Frances Roe realized that "if the Indians should attempt to protect their rights it would be called an uprising at once."[10] All they could do was watch helplessly while the buffalo were destroyed, and, she continued, "all the time they know only too well that with them will go the skins that give them tepees and clothing, and the meat that furnished almost all of their sustenance." Frances Grummond felt "the Indians . . . would fight to the death for home and native land . . . and who would say that their spirit was not commendable and to be respected?"[11]

In general, white women had peaceful relationships with Indians. When coming face to face as women, they probably discovered more in common with their Native American sisters than they liked to admit. One missionary described how Indian women helped her cope after childbirth. Another white woman claimed she only survived the loneliness of her Western home because some Indian women befriended her. Later, she returned their friendship by hiding them from drunken soldiers. When the tribe moved on, the Indian women presented her with a small ring. "No words can express," she claimed, "what that little gold ring meant to me, the love and kindly feeling that was in the hearts of those three Indian women has been a very precious memory to me."[12]

As white people swept across the continent and gobbled up new territories, they didn't worry about whose lands they claimed. Many believed in the United States' destiny to rule North America from the Atlantic to the Pacific. Racial prejudices made the job easy.

The scramble for elbow room and riches came at the expense of Mexican Americans as well as Native Americans. Guidebooks warned of the Mexicans' "ignorance," "superstition," and "barbarity." On a trip down the Santa Fe Trail in 1846, Susan Magoffin expressed surprise about the Mexicans she met. "What a polite people these Mexicans are," she noted in her diary, "altho' they are looked upon as a half-barbarous set by the generality of people." Margaret Hecox traveled to California in 1846 and was terrified that Mexicans would attack her group. Instead, she found that women "came to us as we traveled along . . . bringing us offers of homemade cheese, milk, and other appetizing food."[13]

The avalanche of Anglos pouring into California after the gold rush overwhelmed the Spanish-speaking peoples who'd long called the land home. Luzena Wilson noted the passing of the Spanish land holders in her area of California, her own prejudices showing as she blamed it partly on the "slothfulness and procrastination" of the "Mexican character." But a greater reason, she admitted, lay in the Mexican people's trust of the white newcomers, who cheated them out of their property using high taxes and complicated laws written in English, reducing once proud landowners "from affluence almost to beggary."[14] Threats and violence scared other Mexicans off their land while white settlers stole cattle from Mexican ranchers. In letters, Hispanic women labeled the greedy Americans as "thieves," "murderers," and people "not to be trusted."

By 1848, war and treaties forced Mexico to hand over Texas, California, and New Mexico Territory to the United States. A settlement with Great Britain gave the United States all of Oregon country below the 49th parallel. Huge numbers of white settlers had arrived in the West, planted themselves, and meant to stay. And more kept coming. By 1890, so many people had sought the promise of a better life in the West that historians declared the American frontier officially "closed."

Rachel Parker Plummer and Cynthia Ann Parker

The Captive and the "White Squaw"

Rachel Parker Plummer

As the morning of May 19, 1836, dawned over Parker's Fort in eastern Texas, Rachel Parker Plummer set about the day's business of tending her 14-month-old son, James Pratt. The Parkers, a clan of six families counting about 24 people, had migrated to Texas from Illinois three years earlier, drawn by offers of free land. They'd amassed a holding of thousands of acres and covered a one-acre lot with a log stockade sheltering a cluster of cabins, protected by four blockhouses and an impenetrable front gate. The Parkers' claim lay in a region that was wild and largely unsettled. It was the domain of a fierce warring native people, the Comanche.

That morning, Rachel's husband and father and most of the other men left the fort to work in the cornfields. Seventeen-year-old Rachel, a few months pregnant with her second child, remained behind with the women and children. The protective gate of Parker's Fort stood wide open.

At ten o'clock, a large band of Comanche and a few Kiowa, perhaps 100 mounted men and women, approached the fort. Rachel's uncle, Benjamin Parker, met the group, and in a matter of minutes the sunny morning turned into hell. Rachel watched as the Comanche cut down her uncle, impaled him on lances, clubbed him, shot him with arrows, and peeled back his scalp. She grabbed her son and tried to run but was quickly overtaken, clubbed over the head, and dragged outside to the main group of Indians. Two Comanche women whipped her. "I suppose," Rachel wrote later, "that it was to make me quit crying."[15]

Meanwhile, the Indians killed her Uncle Silas while other Comanche rode down people fleeing the fort—Rachel's grandparents, cousins, and aunts. The Comanche captured Elizabeth Kellogg, Rachel's aunt, and threw her over the back of a horse. The Indians caught Silas Parker's wife, Lucy, dashing with her four children toward the cornfields. They forced Lucy to hand over two of her children, seven-year-old John and her blue-eyed, nine-year-old daughter, Cynthia Ann. Lucy Parker and her remaining children were dragged back toward the fort, but they were saved by men running from the cornfields, shouldering their rifles.

The Comanche galloped north with their captives, two women and three children. Two groups of surviving Parkers ran for their lives toward Fort Houston, a harrowing journey of 65 miles.

The Comanche had raided the southern plains for centuries, unleashing their power against Apache and Ute, against Spaniards and Mexicans, and against the white intruders. The rules were clear enough, and they were brutal: men were killed, and any male captured alive was tortured to death—impaled, scalped, roasted, hacked, shot. Comanche men took turns raping women captives, and some women were further tortured and killed. A young, healthy woman was often kept alive, though, to work as a slave. Babies, useless and needing care, were usually killed, while the Comanche typically adopted older children into the tribe.

The Comanche also ransomed captives for what they prized most—horses. This was the Comanche way, and the way of other warrior societies of the plains. As the white settlers shoved their way onto Indian lands, the brutality on both sides—white and Indian—escalated.

The raid had occurred at ten in the morning. The Comanche, with their captives lashed behind riders, galloped hard until after midnight. After setting up camp, the Indians celebrated with a victory dance around the fire, showing off the dangling scalps of the Parker victims. As part of the ritual, they kicked the captives and beat them with their bows.

The women were stripped naked, their hands tied behind their backs, and their ankles bound. They were thrown face down on the ground, and their hands and feet were pulled together behind them. Rachel feared she'd smother in a pool of her own blood. The three children were also beaten. Rachel later recorded, "Often did the children cry but were soon hushed by blows I had no idea they could survive."[16]

Like all females taken by the Comanche, Rachel and Elizabeth were raped. Rachel passed over this humiliating and painful "degradation" (the 19th-century code word for rape) in her later writing, saying, "To undertake to narrate their barbarous treatment would only add to my present distress, for it is with the feelings of deepest mortification that I think of it, much less to speak or write of it."[17]

For the next five days, the Comanche and the captives rode north, and for five days the Parkers had no food and only enough water to keep them alive. Each night they were bound with leather, face down on the ground, the leather pulled so tight it cut into their flesh.

On the sixth day, the Comanche separated the captives. Elizabeth Kellogg was traded to a band of Kichai Indians. Cynthia Ann and her brother John went to one band of Comanche, while Rachel and James Pratt went to another. They soon tore James from Rachel's arms. "He reached out his hands toward me, which were covered with blood, and cried, "Mother, Mother, oh, Mother!" I looked after him as he was borne from me, and I sobbed aloud. This was the last I ever heard of my little Pratt."[18]

The Comanche took Rachel further north, probably into what is today Colorado. She was given to an older man and became the slave of his wife and daughter, who beat her and burned her. While tending horses and scraping and tanning buffalo hides, she picked up the Comanche language as best she could.

The lowest point of Rachel's existence came after she gave birth in October 1836 to the child she'd been carrying at the time of the raid. Her master felt Rachel's care of the child wasted too much time. One morning, while several men held Rachel back, the Comanche killed her seven-week-old baby. "My little innocent one was not only dead," Rachel later wrote, "but literally torn to pieces."[19]

Every week, the Comanche moved on. At night, the men danced. Rachel listened to tribal councils, watched the rituals, and noted the tribe's taboos. But the harsh life—the loss of her two sons, the work, the abuse—robbed her of hope. She longed to die but couldn't end her own life. She tried instead to goad her Comanche tormentors into killing her. Rachel refused to obey an order from her "young mistress," and when the woman charged at her, Rachel went even further—she fought back. The two women rolled on the ground, fighting and screaming, and Rachel beat the Comanche woman on the head with a buffalo bone until parts of her skull lay exposed. Rachel expected at any second "to feel a spear reach my heart from one of the Indians."[20]

The group of Comanche men gathered around, yelling, but did not interfere in the battle. Rachel emerged victorious. "I had her past hurting me and indeed nearly past breathing, when she cried out for mercy," Rachel wrote.[21] Afterward, Rachel bathed the woman's bloody face, and for the first time, her captor seemed friendly.

The older woman, however, told Rachel she would burn her to death, and Rachel once again fought back. The two women locked in battle inside the teepee, moving over and around a blazing fire that burned them both, and they broke the teepee's lodge pole in the struggle. Twice Rachel held the old woman in the flames before the fight rolled outside the teepee into a crowd of men. No one stopped them, and again Rachel turned the tables on her captor.

Twelve chiefs decided that, as punishment, Rachel would have to replace the broken lodge pole. She refused to do so unless the other two women helped. The council agreed; Rachel was amazed that they'd treated her as an equal. "They respected bravery more than anything, I learned. I wish I had known it sooner," she wrote. "After that, I took up for myself, and fared much the better for it."[22]

Rachel hatched a new plan to escape her captivity. She tried to encourage a Mexican who traded with the Comanche to buy her. "I told him that even if my father and husband were dead, I knew I had enough land in Texas to fully indemnify him; but he did not try to buy me."[23] However, the next time Mexican traders came to the camp, Rachel got the result she'd prayed for: in August 1837, her Comanche master sold her.

The "Comanchero" traders hauled Rachel on a long journey to Santa Fe, which was still part of Mexico at the time. The men had standing orders from a white couple named William and Mary Donoho to offer any price for white women held captive by Indians. The Donohos took Rachel in and promised a swift return to her relatives. But an uprising among the Pueblo Indians forced the Donohos to flee. They trekked right across Comanche country in a two-month journey back to their Missouri home, and Rachel traveled with them.

During Rachel's captivity, her father, James Parker, had followed any tips he'd heard about a white female amongst the Indians. He made five trips between 1836 and 1837 and covered perhaps 5,000 miles in a fruitless search for his lost daughter and grandson. He successfully recovered his sister-in-law, Elizabeth Kellogg, three months after her capture with Rachel and the children, by paying a ransom of $150 to a group of Delaware Indians.

Exhausted after his last search, James sent his son-in-law to visit the Red River trading posts in search of fresh news. Finally, they heard a tip that a Mrs. Plummer had been taken to Independence, Missouri! Rachel's brother-in-law hastened north to find her. As soon as she saw him, she asked, "Are my husband and father alive?" Yes, he told her. Then she asked after her mother and siblings. They too had survived.

Rachel Plummer's ordeals had carried her thousands of miles, crisscrossing the Great Plains. And now, in the dead of winter, she made yet another trek, this time back to Texas. On February 19, 1838, she arrived at her father's home north of Houston. The sight of her shocked everyone. "She presented a most pitiable appearance," noted James Parker, "her emaciated body was covered with scars, the evidence of the savage barbarity to which she had been subject during her captivity."[24]

Rachel's husband must have welcomed his wife home, though this was not always the case with female captives who had been compromised sexually. Though society might pity them, returned female captives usually lived in the shadows of shame. Another female captive, Matilda Lockhart, explained that she had been burned, disfigured, beaten—and had suffered even worse. She'd been "utterly degraded and could not hold her head up again."[25]

But Rachel and her husband soon began another family. She wrote of her ordeal, published as *Rachel Plummer's Narrative of Twenty-One Months Servitude as a Prisoner Among the Comanche Indians*. She not only told of her fate but also described the lands and customs of the Comanche, offering details of their culture during their last free decades on the plains. Rachel's little book proved a sensation.

But Rachel's troubles were not yet over. Late in her pregnancy, vigilantes accused James Parker of murder. He wrote the governor requesting help, for he knew this lawless band had held mock trials and hanged other victims. The threats forced the family to flee their home. Exposure to the elements weakened Rachel, probably nine months pregnant at that point and having never quite recovered from her captivity. She gave birth on January 4, 1839, and died on March 19, followed shortly in death by her infant son.

Rachel Plummer always thought her little boy James Pratt had died. She did not live to see her son returned to the family along with his cousin, John Parker. The boys were found in 1843, ages eight and 13. Now, only one captive from the raid of May 19, 1836, remained missing: John's sister, Cynthia Ann Parker.

Cynthia Ann Parker

Cynthia Ann Parker vanished into the great sea of the plains on that morning in May, ripped from her mother while her father was cut down by Comanche raiders. With the other captives, she endured beatings and starvation in those first terrifying days.

But unlike Rachel Plummer, enslaved and abused, nine-year-old Cynthia Ann found a new home and a new life, adopted into the Comanche world. And there she lived for the next 24 years, forgetting her English language, marrying a Comanche chief and warrior, and bearing three beloved children. Indeed, for nearly 10 years, no white person saw Cynthia Ann or heard a word about her.

Cynthia Ann Parker with her daughter Prairie Flower, around 1862.
Panhandle-Plains Historical Museum, Canyon, Texas

She never left any written record of her life among the Comanche. The best historians can do is base her experiences from age nine until 19 on the stories of two other girls, who, like Cynthia Ann, were abducted during raids and adopted into the tribe. The Comanche stole Bianca Babb, called Banc, in 1866. She saw her mother stabbed, shot with arrows, and scalped, and she witnessed another female captive endure "unspeakable violation, humiliation, and involuntary debasement."[26]

But Bianca was given to a Comanche woman, a widow with no children, who cherished the girl, "never scolded me, and seldom ever corrected me," wrote Babb. On cold winter nights, the woman warmed Bianca before the fire, then wrapped her in a buffalo robe and tucked her into bed. Babb wrote of her "Squaw Mother," "She . . . seemed to care as much for me as if I were her very own child."[27]

Life as part of an extended clan often seemed like a carefree holiday to Bianca. She played, ate informal meals that included spearing meat with skewers, learned to swim, and watched war dances. But there was also work, packing and constantly moving camp, and collecting water and wood. During her seven months of captivity, Babb learned the Comanche language and shared the deprivation of Indian life when there was not enough to eat. But she was treated with kindness, always defended the Comanche in later years, and in 1897, applied for official adoption into the Comanche tribe.

Malinda Ann "Minnie" Caudle's story of her 1868 capture survives in a single interview she gave. When Minnie's two aunts were raped and killed by the Comanche, the Indian woman caring for Minnie shielded her from viewing the horrors. Like Bianca Babb, she was treated with kindness by her adopted mother, who cooked meat just to Minnie's liking and told her stories by the campfire. Like Babb, Minnie was ransomed and returned to her family after six months.

Minnie, too, defended the Comanche as good people. As children, they recognized humanity in the Comanche that white adults—often victims of torture and rape—could not find. Cynthia Ann Parker, who was not ransomed and returned within six months, probably experienced similar treatment based on kindness that grew into a sense of belonging to the tribe.

In the spring of 1846, a Texas Indian agent named Leonard Williams was sent by the US government to invite Comanche chiefs to treaty talks. He had another mission—to find out if the Comanche held any captives in their camp and to purchase those captives if possible. At some point Williams learned that a blue-eyed woman lived in the camp. Could this be the missing Parker girl?

Williams tried to purchase Cynthia Ann's freedom but found his offers adamantly rebuffed. A letter to the commissioner of Indian affairs in Washington reported, "The young woman is claimed by one of the Comanche as his wife. From the influence of her alleged husband, or from her own inclination, she is unwilling to leave the people with whom she associates."[28]

The white world found this explanation—that 19-year-old Cynthia Ann Parker refused to return to white society—a shock. In June 1846, the *Houston Telegraph and Texas Register* reported Williams's meeting, trumpeting the news that "Miss Parker has married an Indian chief and is so wedded to the Indians mode of life that she is unwilling to return to her white kindred." The paper lamented, "Even if she should be restored to her kindred here, she would probably take advantage of the first opportunity and flee away to the wilds of northern Texas."[29]

Cynthia Ann—called Nautdah, meaning "someone found"—lived as the wife of Peta Nocona, a warrior and chief who'd participated in the raid on Parker's Fort in 1836. Her husband owned many horses, giving his family wealth that matched his status as a fearless warrior and able hunter. Cynthia Ann shared her husband with one other wife, a full-blooded Comanche woman.

During her years with the Comanche, Cynthia Ann roamed the Great Plains across Texas and Oklahoma. She lived the hard life of an Indian woman, packing up camp, erecting teepees, butchering buffalo, tanning hides, sewing, and cooking. She shared in what proved to be the beginning of the end for the Comanche, witnessing the dwindling numbers lost through war and white man's diseases like cholera, which swept through Indian villages and killed hundreds. The buffalo herds also dwindled, affecting every aspect of Comanche life.

Cynthia Ann bore Peta Nocona three children. A boy, called Quanah, followed by a second son, Peanuts. Later, she gave birth to a daughter named Prairie Flower. Another sighting of Cynthia Ann in 1851 made first mention of her sons. A final report came in the 1850s from explorer Captain Randolph Marcy. "There is at this time," he wrote, "a white woman among the Middle Comanches, who, with her brother, was captured while they were young children from their father's house. . . . This woman has adopted all the habits and peculiarities of the Comanches; has an Indian husband and children, and cannot be persuaded to leave them."[30]

Throughout the 1850s, Peta Nocona led brutal and bloody raids against isolated white settlements across Texas, hoping to stem the tide of invasion into Comanche country. Some raids even took him into Parker County, named for his wife's kin.

The Comanche had never faced such high stakes before. In the two decades since Cynthia Ann's capture, the number of white settlers in Texas had mushroomed from 15,000 people to more than 600,000. Roads lay where none had once existed, even railroad tracks skimmed across the land. Texas had only three newspapers in 1836 to tell the tale of the Parker raid, but by 1860, 71 papers heralded the latest news. The US government meant to protect this frontier and drive the native people into submission or death in the process.

In November 1860, a posse of men tracked Peta Nocona's raiders deep into Comanche territory, discovering a large village that served as a staging ground for the raids. A full-scale invasion, including Texas Rangers and US soldiers, quickly organized. By the time they reached the camp on December 19, most of the village had vanished; only a few Comanche remained, loading up horses with packs of buffalo meat and preparing to leave. The posse's commander, a 23-year old named Sul Ross, divided his men to block the Indians' retreat and then attacked the camp.

The 60 men surprised the Comanche, a group of only about 15, mostly women and old men, with a few warriors for protection. The fight lasted only moments as soldiers cut down horses, dogs, and Indians. Three Comanche escaped: a lone rider on one horse and two riding together on another horse. Ross, his manservant, and another soldier gave chase. Ross was about to shoot the lone Indian, whom he could now see cradled a small child. The rider pulled up the horse and either opened her shirt to show she was a woman or cried "Americano! Americano!" Whatever happened, Ross did not shoot. He ordered his lieutenant to stay with the woman and rode after the other two Indians, firing and striking the rear rider, another woman, who fell to the ground.

The man in front of her fell too, and after a fight, the warrior was killed. Ross's servant, a Mexican named Anton Martinez who'd lived among the Comanche as a boy, identified the dead man as Peta Nocona. The raid killed twelve Comanche and gained three captives—the woman, the little girl she held, and a boy about age nine. But the soldiers had captured several hundred horses and more than 15,000 pounds of buffalo meat—a great blow to the Comanche, who needed that food for winter.

Ross now made a shocking discovery: the Indian woman with the child had bright blue eyes. He now recognized her as a white woman. At the sight of Peta Nocona's body, the "white squaw" began wailing and weeping. They led her back to the village where soldiers busily looted the campsite and scalped the Indian dead.

The woman told Martinez she had been caught after coming back to search for her boys; she feared her sons were dead. She didn't know that Quanah, about age 12, and Peanuts had escaped safely to the village's new location. With Martinez acting as translator, she told Ross that her father had been killed years ago in battle and she and her brother had been captured. Convinced he'd found the long-lost Cynthia Ann Parker, Ross took her to Fort Cooper, a troublesome journey as the "white squaw" constantly attempted to escape.

Once at Fort Cooper, officials questioned her. Cynthia Ann gave a credible report of the raid on Parker's Fort and her father's death. The post commander's wife took charge of cleaning up the filthy woman, who refused to give up her Comanche clothes. Meanwhile, Ross sent for Cynthia Ann's uncle, Isaac Parker, to verify her identity.

When Parker arrived, a desolate woman sat on a pine box with her elbows on her knees and her head in her hands. She ignored the room full of men until Isaac spoke her name. At that, she stood and patted her breast. "Me Cincee Ann," she said. After that, she answered questions about the long-ago raid, remembering much of what had happened. She used a stick to draw an outline of Parker's Fort, which Isaac claimed was a better picture than he could have made himself.

Once more, Cynthia Ann Parker was ripped abruptly and brutally into a foreign world. She had lost her husband and her beloved boys; she felt not rescued but like a captive, shrouded in unbearable sadness. Isaac Parker headed home with Cynthia Ann and Prairie Flower, along with Anton Martinez who served as an interpreter. Now cleaned up and considered presentable, the woman and child were sat on display like a carnival sideshow outside the general store in Fort Worth. A large crowd gathered to gawk. The idea that a little white girl had turned into a savage—abandoning her language and her religion, and bearing the children of a red-skinned brute—proved tantalizing stuff.

Cynthia Ann reacted to her reentry into the white world with hostility or despair; hours passed in weeping and nursing her baby. She tried to run away, and Isaac locked her in the house when he wasn't home. She refused to speak English and refused to give up her Comanche ways. One relative described Cynthia Ann's means of worship:

> She went out to a smooth place on the ground, cleaned it off very nicely and made a circle and a cross. On the cross she built a fire, burned some tobacco, and then cut a place on her breast and let the blood drop onto the fire. She then lit her pipe and blowed smoke toward the sun and assumed an attitude of the most sincere devotion. She afterwards said through an interpreter that this was her prayer to her great spirit to enable her to understand and appreciate that these were her relatives and kindred she was among.[31]

The family insisted that she give up Indian clothes and that Prairie Flower be taught the Bible, but Cynthia Ann remained determined not to change. Isaac took his niece to Austin where he won a pension for her from the Texas legislature. The trip upset her, with everyone staring, and she believed the congressmen were debating whether she should live or die. She tried to run away but was tackled and brought back. The legislature agreed to grant her more than 4,000 acres of land and $100 a year for five years. The money would be held in a trust for her by two Parker cousins.

Cynthia Ann's repeated attempts to escape and her refusal to change led to new living arrangements. She began making the rounds of Parker relatives, moving farther and farther east—away from the plains, away from her sons, and away from any hope of escaping back to her Comanche life.

People came to see her, the famous rescued captive. Cynthia Ann spoke Spanish or Comanche, mixing the two languages as she talked. She tried to bribe one man who spoke the Indian language, promising that she would give him horses, guns, even wives—whatever he wanted—if he would take her back to the Comanche. "My heart is crying all the time for my two sons," she told the man, begging him to take her with him.[32]

At her brother Silas's house, her misery and escape attempts continued, especially as Silas's wife punished Prairie Flower for calling her mother by her Comanche name. She slashed her arms and breasts in mourning and used a butcher knife to chop off her long hair. Around this time, a Fort Worth photographer took the famous picture of Cynthia Ann nursing Prairie Flower.

When Cynthia Ann finally came to her sister Orlena's home, she seemed to at last find some peace and began adjusting to her new life. She learned the housewifery skills of a white woman—weaving, spinning, and sewing. She also tanned hides, a skill she'd mastered as a Comanche. She and Prairie Flower began speaking English.

But Cynthia Ann still hid from gawkers and spent hours crying. She never abandoned some of her Comanche ways, especially the mourning rituals of cutting and keening. One neighbor told of how she still cried for her boys, and another wrote, "I don't think she ever knew but that her sons were killed. And to hear her tell of the happy days of the Indian dances and see the excitement and pure joy which [showed] on her face, the memory of it, I am convinced that the white people did more harm by keeping her away from that then the Indians did by taking her at first."[33]

In 1864, Cynthia Ann suffered another shattering blow when Prairie Flower died of influenza and pneumonia. Little is known of Cynthia Ann's life in the six years that followed. She died in 1870 of influenza, her death perhaps hastened by her starving herself. She never knew that her handsome son Quanah became one of the great Native American warrior chiefs, who never forgot the mother snatched from his life when he was just a twelve-year-old boy.

Quanah Parker.
Library of Congress

Sarah Winnemucca

Life Among the Paiutes

Named Thocmetony (Shell Flower) at birth, Sarah Winnemucca was born in the year 1844, welcomed into a band of Paiute that roamed the deserts of northern Nevada. "I was a very small child when the first white people came into our country," Sarah recalled. "They came like a lion, yes, like a roaring lion, and have continued so ever since, and I have never forgotten their first coming."[34] Sarah's grandfather, Chief Truckee, welcomed the white men as brothers, but for Sarah, the coming of the settlers changed forever how she and her people lived.

Over the next several years, emigrant bands of white settlers and gold-diggers streaming through Paiute land committed crimes against Sarah's people. In one instance, white men burned the band's winter supplies; another time, a group fired on a Paiute fishing party near the Humboldt River, killing one of Sarah's uncles and setting off a ritual of mourning through the village.

The never-ceasing pressure for Paiute lands from white settlers eventually forced Sarah's people onto reservations, first at Pyramid Lake in Nevada, which was followed by treks to far-off reservations in Oregon and finally Yakima, Washington. Over the years, as the government drove the Paiute from one place to another, Sarah lost nearly half her family. She devoted her life, while straddling two worlds, to defending the rights of her Paiute people and to forging an understanding between Indians and the US government.

Years later, Sarah wrote about her youth and the lessons she learned as a child. "Be kind to all, both poor and rich, and feed

Sarah Winnemucca.
Nevada Historical Society

all that come to your wigwam," she wrote, "and your name can be spoken of by every one far and near. In this way you will make many friends for yourself. Be kind both to bad and good, for you don't know your own heart. This is the way my people teach their children. It was handed down from father to son for many generations. I have never in my life saw our children rude as I have seen white children and grown people in the streets."

As a young teen, in 1859, Sarah learned English while living in the household of William Ormsby near Genoa, Nevada. She possessed a gift for languages and spoke several Indian dialects as well as English and some Spanish. During the early 1860s, Sarah lived with her parents and siblings at the Pyramid Lake reservation, on traditional Paiute lands. The government promised the Indians clothes, food, and farm tools, in exchange for the Paiute remaining on the reservation and replacing their old ways of hunting and fishing with farming.

But after the first year, a series of agents issued nothing to the Indians. The tribe dug a ditch for a new mill, but the government-issued money, which was meant to build a gristmill and sawmill, never built a thing for the Indians. White people squatted on the Paiute reservation and set their cattle to graze on the land. Worse, soldiers came and accused the hungry Paiute of stealing cattle from white settlers. The soldiers found a camp of Indians and "killed almost all the people that were there. Oh, it is a fearful thing to tell," Sarah wrote, "but it must be told. . . . I had one baby brother killed there. . . . Yet my people kept peaceful."

Sarah's father suffered greatly at the death of his baby son, going off alone into the hills. Not long after, Sarah's mother and sister died. Incidents of betrayal, misunderstanding, and retaliation between Indians and whites haunted the Paiute. Both sides often turned to Sarah to translate and interpret between the soldiers and agents and her people. On at least one occasion, her efforts won food for the tribe.

But Indian agents repeatedly cheated the Paiute, selling goods meant for the tribe to enrich themselves and giving well-paying jobs to relatives while their Indian charges starved. Sarah reported one issue of goods to weary people who'd traveled three days to reach the agency. A family group of 23 people received four blankets, three fish hooks and lines, and two kettles. "It was the saddest affair I ever saw," she wrote. If the Paiute raised five sacks of grain, she wrote, "they give one sack for the Big Father [*the president*] in Washington; if they have only three sacks, they still have to send one. Every fourth load of hay goes to the Big Father at Washington, yet he does not give my people the seed." Instead, the Paiute had to pay for the seed themselves.

Conditions became so bad that Paiute leaders asked Sarah to travel to San Francisco and meet with the region's commanding military officer. General McDowell reported the Paiute's crooked agent, but the man was not removed. Sarah made more trips to the military commanders over the years, seeking justice for her people, but after receiving promises from the generals, she usually never heard another word from them. She blamed unscrupulous agents for allowing the murder of her people and the loss of their reservation lands. "And yet we, who are called blood-seeking savages, are keeping our promises to the government," she wrote. "Oh, my dear good Christian people, how long are you going to stand by and see us suffer at your hands?"

In the 1870s, the government moved the Paiute to the Malheur Reservation in Oregon. There Sarah worked with the wife of the tribe's fair-minded Indian agent, Samuel Parrish, to open a school. But her joy in the school proved short lived. A new agent replaced Parrish in 1876. He gathered the tribe and had

Sarah translate his mission: he'd come to "make you all good people." He told the Paiute they lived on government land. "If you do well and are willing to work for government, government will give you work," Sarah later recalled his words. But the Paiute knew this land had been promised to them. The land *was* theirs, and what they did on it was theirs.

The new agent quickly set the tone for future dealings. "When I tell you to do anything," Sarah translated, "I don't want any of you to dictate to me, but to go and do it." The Paiute worked for a week, but when they went to get their pay, the agent charged them for any supplies they'd used and refused to pay them in cash. The government, of course, had meant the supplies for Paiute use, without charge. Continued unfair and cruel treatment led some Paiutes to abandon the reservation and join the neighboring Bannock tribe in a war against the government.

In 1878, the army hired Sarah to work as an interpreter, messenger, and scout. They wanted her to persuade the Bannocks to give up. When Sarah reached the Bannock camp, she discovered some Paiutes, including several family members, whom she later claimed were being held captive. She told them that the army approached and they must flee. She left with the Paiute, and they hid in the hills from the Bannocks while Sarah galloped ahead to get help from the soldiers, riding 200 miles over two sleepless days and nights.

Sarah continued in the army's service for the rest of the Bannock War. The insurrection ended when General Oliver Otis Howard captured about 1,000 Bannocks and killed 140 men, women, and children at Charles's Ford, Wyoming, in September 1878.

But Sarah's efforts won no concessions for her tribe. The government punished all Paiutes, not only the ones who'd joined the Bannock, with removal to a new reservation at Yakima in Washington Territory. The nightmare journey, in the icy depths of winter, killed many members of the already half-starved tribe. They arrived at the new agency on the last day of December 1878, mourning the loss of children who had frozen to death in the deep snows. The agent issued them goods—"Oh, such a heart-sickening issue!" lamented Sarah—a few shawls and a few yards of cloth so poor for sewing clothes that "you white people would sift flour through" it.

Many Paiute died that winter. Sarah's sister lingered, suffering with illness, and died in the spring. Though Sarah kept working for the government as an interpreter, her disgust at the treatment of her people led to a greater step—she would speak for the Paiutes on a larger stage.

In January 1880, Sarah began her work as an activist for her people, pleading their cause before the secretary of the interior, Carl Schurz, in Washington, DC. The secretary made her many promises he never kept, and some Paiutes blamed Sarah for the government's lies. Some believed she took money from the agents or sold them out to the soldiers, causing the move to Yakima. At one point, when Yakima agent "Father" James Wilbur threatened to throw her in jail for rabble rousing, Sarah wished he would, "for that would have made my people see that I had not sold them."

In 1882, she married Lewis Hopkins, an Indian Department employee. A year later, they traveled east, and Sarah began a tireless round of lectures—more than 300 presentations—on behalf of the Paiute, sponsored in part by Mrs. Horace Mann, wife of the celebrated reformer. Then, in 1883, Sarah penned and published her autobiography, the first book by a Native American woman, called *Life Among the Piutes: Their Wrongs and Claims*. Sarah not only wrote of the wrongs done to her people by a corrupt government system of agents but also told the story of growing up in her native culture, showing Indian life from an Indian perspective, a personal account that had not been written before.

When Hopkins died in 1887, Sarah devoted herself to opening a school for Indian children in Nevada. She fought for her students to remain near their parents instead of being taken away to boarding schools where much of their Indian heritage and language would be obliterated. Sarah believed in taking certain skills of white culture, like writing, and adopting them for her people's use.

Sarah kept her school open for four years, but her dream withered from lack of funding. She moved to live with her younger sister, Elma, in Montana, where she died on October 17, 1891. Sarah Winnemucca is remembered today as a compassionate woman who sought understanding between two nations and cultures, and fought for the heritage of her people.

Susette La Flesche

"An Indian Is a Person"

"How often I have fallen asleep when a child," wrote Susette La Flesche, "with my arms tight around my grandmother's neck, while she told me a story. . . . When thinking of those old days—so happy and free, when we slept night after night in a tent on the wide trackless prairie, with nothing but the skies above us and the earth beneath; with nothing to make us afraid; not even knowing that we were not civilized, or were ordered to be by the government; not even knowing that there were such beings

Susette La Flesche. *Nebraska State Historical Society*

as white men; happy in our freedom and our love for each other—I often wonder if there is anything in your civilization which will make good to us what we have lost."[35]

Her blood mingled white and Indian ancestry. Susette La Flesche, bearing both the name of French ancestors and her Indian name, Inshtatheumba, or Bright Eyes, straddled both worlds as she advocated for the rights of her Native American people.

In 1854, the year of Susette's birth, her father Joseph, also called Iron Eyes, signed a treaty with the United States. The government promised their tribe, the Omaha, would keep 300,000 acres of their traditional lands in eastern Nebraska for their reservation. Government Indian agents would run the reservation, hand out money, and provide food and clothes. Joseph believed the only way for the Omaha to survive the surging waves of white settlers was to adopt the farming lifestyle of the whites. The Indian practice of communal sharing would have to give way to the self-interest of the individual.

As a child, Susette learned about Christianity and how to write, read, and speak English at the reservation's mission school. A former mission teacher won Susette a spot at a private school for young ladies in New Jersey. She graduated in June 1875 and returned to the reservation. For three years, Susette tried to secure a position teaching but was thwarted by dealings with Indian agents and government red tape. Eventually she won a job as an assistant teacher.

The years had been difficult for the Omaha and other Indian tribes. The invasion of white settlers carried soldiers in its wake, followed by railroads and by hunters who killed buffalo for the skins and tongues, leaving the meat to rot. The animal central to the lives of the Plains Indians edged ever closer to the brink of extinction. Corrupt agents pocketed tribal funds and paid the tribes in shoddy goods. Hunger and suffering haunted once proud Indian nations.

But even worse for the northern tribes was the threat of removal south to Indian Territory, an arid, harsh land in present-day Oklahoma. In 1877, this happened to the Omaha's close friends, the Ponca. Joseph's mother was a Ponca, and his brother, White Swan, grew up with that tribe. Armed with her education, her ability to translate, and her skill with a pen, Susette became deeply involved in the Ponca's plight.

Like the Omaha, in the 1850s the peaceful Ponca turned over thousands of acres to the United States. They welcomed a mission church to their reservation, worked their fields, and built log houses. But the government rewarded the Ponca's cooperation by doling out only a fraction of the supplies and money promised them.

Then, in 1868, the government mistakenly handed over the Ponca's "permanent" homeland to another tribe—the Sioux. In May 1877, soldiers drove 700 Ponca, "as one would drive a herd of ponies," south to Indian Territory. Susette and Joseph met the Ponca en route—and the sight broke Susette's heart. For those few days, she heard the Ponca cries for their dead and cries for their old home. The visit haunted her.

Nearly 150 Ponca died of disease and hunger during the first year in Oklahoma. Later, Susette traveled to Indian Territory to report firsthand on the Ponca's stark living conditions. And all the time she worried, If this could happen to the Ponca, and so many other tribes, why not the Omaha?

Susette plied her pen in letters to the president, the secretary of the interior, and the Indian commissioner. She wrote for herself and translated the words of others. "Because I am an Indian can you order me to the Indian Territory, New Mexico, or any place you please, and I be powerless to appeal to any law for protection?" she asked the commissioner.[36] But of course, the government could do as it wished.

Then, in January 1879, Ponca chief Standing Bear and about 30 others fled the reservation and headed north toward their homelands in Nebraska. Standing Bear's dying son had begged to be taken back to the land of their fathers. After a grueling 10-week winter journey that left them sick and nearly starved, Standing Bear's refugees arrived at the Omaha reservation. Joseph believed that, once the Ponca settled on Omaha lands, everything would work out. But soon soldiers under the command of General George Crook arrived to arrest the runaway Ponca and take them to the fort at Omaha.

Susette and the Omahas waited for word about Standing Bear and his people. They expected to hear they'd been shipped back to Indian Territory. But instead, word came that the Ponca had a champion, a journalist named Thomas H. Tibbles, who'd interviewed Standing Bear and telegraphed his story to papers around the country. Tibbles also enlisted the aid of lawyers John

Webster and A. J. Poppleton to bring against General Crook a writ of *habeas corpus*, which required that a prisoner be brought before a court to decide the legality of his imprisonment.

Tibbles wrote to the physician at the Omaha reservation, asking for all information about the Ponca incident. The doctor had Susette write her chronicle of events instead. "This statement," she finished, "shows how much they trusted in the justice of the white people, believing that the wrong done to them had been done by only a few, and without authority. I do hope some action will be taken in the matter soon."[37]

The government responded that Indians were "not persons within the meaning of the law" and possessed no rights protected under the Constitution. Indians stood as wards of the government, like children under their parents. No attorney could appear for an Indian unless authorized by the Indian Department. Commissioner Hays defended the Ponca's removal, claiming that it was obviously necessary once their land had been given to the Sioux. "If the reservation system is to be maintained," he wrote, "discontented and restless or mischievous Indians cannot be permitted to leave their reservations at will and go where they please."[38]

Susette received permission from the Omaha agent to travel to Omaha and sat beside Joseph in the back of the courtroom during Standing Bear's trial. In May 1880, Susette heard Judge Elmer Dundy's ruling that "an Indian is a person within the meaning of the laws of the United States" and could not be forcibly moved or confined without giving his consent.

The legal victory—recognition of Native American rights to personal freedom and protection under the US Constitution—proved a double-edged win. Standing Bear and his small band won the right to remain in Nebraska, but the other Ponca in Indian Territory could not move. The government made clear that the case only applied to Standing Bear and his band; no other Indians could leave their reservations.

Susette returned to her teaching, but Tibbles and others urged her to join a speaking tour of Eastern cities. News that a bill had been introduced in Congress to remove the Omaha spurred her to overcome her stage fright and shyness and take action. With her brother Francis, Standing Bear, and Tibbles, Susette undertook an exhausting speaking tour to drum up support for the Ponca and stop further forced removals of Indians from their homelands. Susette worked as Standing Bear's interpreter and also spoke to huge crowds in cities including Chicago, New York, Philadelphia, and Boston, where she became the first woman to speak at historic Faneuil Hall.

Papers latched onto Susette's romantic sounding Indian name—Bright Eyes—and described her as intelligent, sweet, graceful, and lovely, a "dusky Indian maiden" wearing a plain black silk dress. "No such interesting squaw has appeared since Pocahontas," noted the *Ladies Journal*.[39] On meeting her, Henry Wadsworth Longfellow declared he had found his flesh and blood Minnehaha—the Indian girl in his epic poem *The Song of Hiawatha*.

In interviews and speeches, Susette demanded fair and honest treatment of native people. She asked that Indians be allowed to remain on their lands—lands that had been deeded to them by formal treaties later broken by the United States government. She wanted Indians to have a say in how the government spent money meant for the tribes. She decried that the government kept soldiers on reservations to put down disturbances incited by injustices and that an Indian could be arrested without trial and sent away.

"When the Indian, being a man and not a child or a thing, or merely an animal, as some would-be civilizers have termed him, fights for his property, liberty, and life, they call him a savage," Susette wrote. She denounced the corrupt reservation system as a "system of nursing and feeding," which prevented Indians from earning their own livings and taking care of themselves.[40] Within that system, many tribes faced starvation. Then the government turned around and claimed Indians were incapable of taking care of themselves and would starve if the government left them alone.

"This system has been tried for nearly a hundred years and has only worked ruin for the Indian," Susette argued. Instead, give the Indian title to his lands, "throw over him the protection of the law," and grant Indians the rights of citizenship.[41]

She appeared before Congressional committees, expressing her views on the treatment of Native Americans and the Ponca removal. She met president Rutherford B. Hayes, his wife, senators, and other dignitaries. Susette's work inspired others, including Helen Hunt Jackson, who wrote *A Century of Dishonor* about the government's betrayal of Indian treaties, and Massachusetts senator Henry Dawes, who sponsored the Dawes Act of 1887, which broke up the reservation system and instead granted plots of land to individual Indians to farm as homesteaders.

In 1882, Susette married Tibbles, now a widower. The two continued lecture tours of the east and in 1886 traveled to England and Scotland, where Susette was hailed as an "Indian Princess," much to her embarrassment. Back home, they divided their time between living on the reservation and in Omaha, where Tibbles worked as an editor.

Though Susette believed Native Americans must learn to farm as white men did, she also wrote for children's magazines about traditional Omaha life and legends, drawing illustrations of playing children, cradleboards, teepees, drying buffalo meat, and clothing. "We camp no more in the great circle," she lamented. "A few of the old men only remember our laws and customs and try to keep them. The young are passing into another life."[42]

In late 1891, Tibbles and Susette traveled to Pine Ridge, one of the Sioux reservations in southwestern South Dakota. Many had fled the reservation, fearful of the soldiers who'd come to quell any disturbances aroused by the Ghost Dance. Starving Indians danced to bring the savior, to see departed loved ones living again, and to see the whites driven away and a new earth returned, once again home to free Indians, the buffalo, the elk, and the antelope.

On Christmas Eve, soldiers slaughtered a band of Indians camped near Wounded Knee Creek; they were under Chief Big Foot and included men, women, and children. In one of the darkest moments of her life, Susette helped care for the survivors that escaped to Pine Ridge.

Beginning in 1893, the Tibbles lived in Washington, DC, for two years, while Susette worked to save Omaha lands before returning once more to Nebraska. Tibbles turned his attention from Indian affairs to the Populist political movement. Susette continued to write and draw and advocate for Indians. The lands once promised to the Omaha were openly signed away to greedy whites who wanted surplus lands not yet rationed in allotments to the tribe. Instead of teaching and helping the Omaha, the government still controlled and doled out money.

During her last years, Susette worried she had saved her people from leaving their homeland, only to see Omaha lands wasted away. The 300,000 acres promised the Omaha in 1854 had dwindled to 30,000 acres. Susette struggled with illness, and in 1902 her sister Susan, a medical school–trained physician, helped care for her.

Susette La Flesche died on May 26, 1903, only 49 years old, a shy, soft-spoken woman who'd overcome her fears to boldly champion the cause of Native Americans through her pen and eloquent voice.

7

LOVE SONG TO THE WEST

How often at night
When the heavens are bright
With the lights from the glittering stars
Have I stood here amazed and asked as I gazed
If their glory exceeds that of ours.
—Second verse, "Home on the Range"

As a new bride, Frances Boyd regarded her New York City home as "the only habitable place on the globe." In 1868, however, she joined her soldier-husband in the wild Southwest. Seventeen years later, a life of privation and hardship could not dampen Boyd's appreciation for the West. "Oh, I love the West," she wrote, "and dislike to think that the day will surely come when it will teem with human life and all its warring elements!"[1]

On a yearlong visit back to New York, Boyd "raved about the delights of the West until friends thought me nearly crazy

Female daredevils, Kitty Tatch and friend, at Yosemite Valley in California.
National Park Service, Historic Photograph Collection

on the subject."[2] She proclaimed New York's Catskill Mountains "insipid after the rocky grandeur of the west,"[3] and deplored New York City's endless turmoil and chimneys blocking out the sky. Years later, returning east as a widow, Frances Boyd never forgot the blue-domed skies and grand spaces of the Southwest, where, she wrote, "one is truly alone with God."[4]

Many women echoed Boyd's celebration of beauty, freedom, and joy in the West. "The air is so exhilarating," enthused Elizabeth Custer, "one feels as if he had never breathed a full breath before."[5] A Kansas woman described her new home in 1859:

> It was such a new world, reaching to the far horizon without break of tree or chimney stack; just sky and grass and grass and sky. . . . The hush was so loud. As I lay in my unplastered upstairs room, the heavens seemed nearer than ever before and awe and beauty and mystery over all.[6]

"It might seem a cheerless life," claimed another woman,

> but there were many compensations: the thrill of conquering a new country; the wonderful atmosphere; the attraction of the prairie, which simply gets into your blood and makes you dissatisfied away from it; the low-lying hills and the unobstructed view of the horizon; and the fleecy clouds driven by the never failing winds.[7]

Award-winning author Willa Cather portrayed the Western land as a powerful force in her stories. Many pioneering women shared the same tug at their souls, the sense of themselves, the sense of change that Cather expressed:

> It was over flat lands like this, stretching out to drink the sun, that the larks sang—and one's heart sang there too. . . . There was a new song in that blue air which had never been sung in the world before.[8]

NOTES

Chapter 1: Many a Weary Mile

1. Lillian Schlissel, *Women's Diaries of the Westward Journey* (New York: Schocken Books, 1982), 55. Idiosyncratic grammar, spelling, and punctuation have been retained in quoted material here and throughout the book.
2. Julie Roy Jeffrey, *Frontier Women: The Trans-Mississippi West 1840–1880* (New York: Hill and Wang, 1979), 31.
3. Luzena Stanley Wilson. *'49er: Her Memoirs as Taken Down by Her Daughter in 1881*, http://www.pbs.org/weta/thewest/resources/archives/three/luzena.htm.
4. Sandra Myres, *Westering Women and the Frontier Experience, 1800–1915* (Albuquerque: University of New Mexico Press, 1982), 27.
5. Schlissel, *Women's Diaries*, 72.
6. Wilson, *'49er*, 1.
7. Catherine Haun, quoted in Schlissel, *Women's Diaries*, 168.
8. Myres, *Westering Women*, 25.
9. Maria Shrode, quoted in Myres, *Westering Women*, 138.
10. Schlissel, *Women's Diaries*, 78.
11. Helen Carpenter, quoted in Myres, *Westering Women*, 123.
12. Schlissel, *Women's Diaries*, 81.

13. Amelia Stewart Knight, *Diary of Mrs. Amelia Stewart Knight* (1853), http://www.oregontrail101.com/00.ar.knight.html.
14. Ibid.
15. Jane Kellogg, quoted in Schlissel, *Women's Diaries*, 59.
16. Lucy Henderson (ibid., 49).
17. Ibid., 51.
18. Missionary Mary Walker, 1838, quoted in Cathy Luchetti and Carol Olwell, *Women of the West* (New York: Orion Books, 1982), 129.
19. Knight, *Diary.*
20. Jeffrey, *Frontier Women*, 48.
21. Jane Gould Tourtillott, 1862, quoted in Schlissel, *Women's Diaries*, 227.
22. Knight, *Diary.*
23. Virginia Reed Murphy, *Across the Plains in the Donner Party: A Personal Narrative of the Overland Trip to California*, http://www.teleport.com/~mhaller/Primary/VReed/VReed1.html.
24. Ethan Rarick, *Desperate Passage: The Donner Party's Perilous Journey West* (New York: Oxford University Press. 2008), 77.
25. Murphy, *Across the Plains.*
26. Rarick, *Desperate Passage*, 174.
27. Murphy, *Across the Plains.*
28. Rarick, *Desperate Passage*, 200.
29. Rarick, *Desperate Passage*, 229.
30. All quotes in this passage come from *Diary of Mrs. Amelia Stewart Knight (1853).* The journal is also included in part in Schlissel, *Women's Diaries*, 201–16.

Chapter 2: Oh, Give Me a Home

1. Frances Carrington, *My Army Life: A Soldier's Wife at Fort Phil Kearny* (1910; repr., Boulder, CO: Pruett Publishing, 1990), 57.
2. Schlissel, *Women's Diaries*, 148.
3. Mary Ballou, 1852, quoted in Christiane Fischer, ed., *Let Them Speak for Themselves: Women in the American West, 1849–1900* (Hamden, CT: Archon Book, 1977), 43.
4. Abby Mansur, quoted in Fisher, *Let Them Speak*, 49.

5. Miriam Davis Colt, *Went to Kansas,* 1862, http://www.kancoll.org/books/colt.
6. Schlissel, *Women's Diaries,* 157.
7. Walker Wyman, *Frontier Woman: The Life of a Woman Homesteader on the Dakota Frontier* (River Falls: University of Wisconsin Press, 1972), 16.
8. Carrie Lassell Detrick, quoted in Joanna L. Stratton, *Pioneer Women: Voices from the Kansas Frontier* (New York: Simon and Schuster, 1981), 55.
9. Ibid., 53.
10. Myres, *Westering Women,* 86.
11. Willa Cather, *My Ántonia* (1918; repr., Boston: Houghton Mifflin, 1954), 29.
12. Dorothy Gray, *Women of the West* (Millbrae, CA: Les Femmes Press, 1976), 140.
13. Lydia Lyons, quoted in Stratton, *Pioneer Women,* 52.
14. Virginia Wilcox Ivins, quoted in Fischer, *Let Them Speak,* 76.
15. Marguerite Merington, *The Custer Story: The Life and Intimate Letters of General George A. Custer and His Wife Elizabeth* (New York: Devin-Adair, 1950), 81.
16. Merington, *Custer Story,* 211.
17. Frances Boyd, *Cavalry Life in Tent and Field* (1894; repr., Lincoln: University of Nebraska Press, 1982), 45.
18. Elizabeth Custer, *Following the Guidon* (repr., Norman: University of Oklahoma Press, 1966), 239.
19. Boyd, 144.
20. Elizabeth Custer, *Boots and Saddles, or Life in Dakota With General Custer* (1885; repr., Norman: University of Oklahoma Press, 1961), 105.
21. Elizabeth Custer, *Tenting on the Plains* (repr., Norman: University of Oklahoma Press, 1971), 2: 485.
22. Carrington, *My Army Life,* 86.
23. Virginia Wilcox Ivins, quoted in Fischer, *Let Them Speak,* 77.
24. Mary Jane Megquier, 1849, quoted in Schlissel, *Women's Diaries,* 62.
25. Julie Roy Jeffrey, *Converting the West: A Biography of Narcissa Whitman* (Norman: University of Oklahoma Press, 1991), 37. Many

Whitman sources, including some of Narcissa's letters, can be seen at the website for the Whitman Mission National Park, http://nps.gov/whmi/historyculture/narcissa-biography.htm.

26. Ibid., 69.
27. Ibid., 63.
28. Ibid., 76–77.
29. Ibid., 81.
30. Ibid., 83.
31. Ibid., 98.
32. Ibid., 106.
33. Ibid.
34. Ibid., 119.
35. Ibid.
36. Ibid., 126.
37. Ibid., 145
38. Ibid., 149.
39. Ibid., 147.
40. Ibid., 177.
41. Ibid.
42. Ibid., 203.
43. Ibid.
44. Ibid., 215.
45. Ibid.
46. All quotes in this passage come from Miriam Davis Colt's book, *Went to Kansas*, published in 1862, which is also included in part in Luchetti and Olwell, *Women of the West*.
47. All quotes in this passage come from Frances Grummond Carrington's book, *My Army Life*.

Chapter 3: A Woman That Can Work

1. Schlissel, *Women's Diaries*, 64.
2. Mary Ballou, quoted in Fischer, *Let Them Speak*, 44.
3. Mary Jane Megquire, quoted in Schlissel, *Women's Diaries*, 62.
4. Anne Butler, *Daughters of Joy, Sisters of Misery: Prostitutes in the American West, 1865–90* (Chicago: University of Chicago Press, 1985), 10.

5. Mary Walker, 1840, quoted in Luchetti and Olwell, 68, 70.
6. Paula Bartley and Cathy Loxton, *Plains Women: Women in the American West* (Cambridge: Cambridge University Press, 1991), 31.
7. Elinore Stewart, quoted in Myres, *Westering Women*, 163.
8. Mathilda Wagner, quoted in Bartley and Loxton, *Plains Women*, 24.
9. Mary Walker, quoted in Luchetti and Olwell, *Women of the West*, 71.
10. Myres, *Westering Women*, 152.
11. Susan Armitage and Elizabeth Jameson, *The Women's West* (Norman: University of Oklahoma Press, 1987), 186.
12. Martha Summerhayes, *Vanished Arizona: Recollections of My Army Life* (1908; repr., New York: J. B. Lippincott, 1963).
13. All quotes in this passage are from Luzena Stanley Wilson's book, *'49er: Her Memoirs as Taken Down by Her Daughter in 1881.* For the "untold" side of the story, see Fern Henry, *My Checkered Life: Luzena Stanley Wilson in Early California* (Nevada City, CA: Carl Mautz Publishing, 2003). Henry's book looks more deeply into the background of Luzena's story and what else happened to her.
14. Kathleen Bruyn, *"Aunt" Clara Brown: Story of a Black Pioneer* (Boulder: Pruett Publishing, 1971), 159. This biography is marred by lengthy fictionalized sections and heavy use of "negro dialect."
15. Ibid., preface, xiii.
16. All quotes in this passage are from Bethenia Owens-Adair's book, *Dr. Owens-Adair: Some of Her Life Experiences*, 1906, as printed in Luchetti and Olwell, *Women of the West*, 173–87.

Chapter 4: And Now the Fun Begins

1. Rebecca Craver, *The Impact of Intimacy: Mexican-Anglo Intermarriage in New Mexico, 1821–1846* (El Paso: Texas Western Press, 1982), 23.
2. Ibid., 13.
3. Harriet Behrins, quoted in Fischer, *Let Them Speak*, 29.
4. Abby Mansur (ibid., 52).
5. Custer, *Boots*, 101.
6. Wilson, *'49er.*

7. "Adah Menken, aka 'the Naked Lady': The Original Superstar," Michael Foster and Barbara Foster, http://www.historynet.com/adah-menken-aka-the-naked-lady-the-original-superstar.htm.
8. "Adah Isaacs Menken, 1835–68," Jewish Women Archive Encyclopedia, http://jwa.org/encyclopedia/article/menken-adah-isaacs.
9. Joan Severa, *Dressed for the Photographer: Ordinary Americans and Fashion 1840–1900* (Kent, Ohio: Kent State University Press, 1995), 298.
10. Harriet Carr (ibid., 88).
11. Schlissel, *Women's Diaries*, 125.
12. Custer, *Tenting*, 2: 405.
13. Craver, *Impact of Intimacy*, 24.
14. Miriam Colt, *Went to Kansas*.
15. Agnes Morley Cleveland, quoted in Grace, *Carry A. Nation*, 113.
16. Belknap's journal, in Luchetti and Olwell, *Women of the West*, 138.
17. Rachel Haskell, quoted in Jeffrey, *Frontier Women*, 129.
18. Fischer, *Let Them Speak*, 59.
19. Keturah Belknap, quoted in Luchetti and Olwell, *Women of the West*, 139.
20. Myres, *Westering Women*, 203.
21. Glenda Riley, *The Female Frontier: A Comparative View of Women on the Prairie and the Plains* (Lawrence: University Press of Kansas, 1988), 174.
22. Maxine Benson, *Martha Maxwell, Rocky Mountain Naturalist* (Lincoln: University of Nebraska Press, 1986), 55.
23. Benson, *Martha Maxwell*, 38.
24. Ibid., 39.
25. Ibid., 57.
26. Ibid., 69.
27. Ibid., 75.
28. Ibid., 82.
29. Ibid., 85.
30. Ibid., 231.
31. Ibid., 88.
32. Ibid., 95.
33. Ibid., 119.
34. Ibid., 132.

35. Ibid., 137.
36. Ibid., 147.
37. Ibid., 159.
38. Ibid., 174.
39. David Dempsey, *The Triumphs and Trials of Lotta Crabtree* (New York: William Morrow, 1968), 148.
40. Ibid., 162.
41. Ibid., 187.
42. Ibid., 186.
43. Ibid., 235.

Chapter 5: Great Expectations for the Future

1. Gray, *Women of the West*, 53.
2. Jeffrey, *Frontier Women*, 130.
3. Ibid., 8.
4. Stratton, *Pioneer Women*, 58.
5. Grace Fairchild, quoted in Wyman, *Frontier Woman*, 31.
6. Riley, *Female Frontier*, 186.
7. Jeffrey, *Frontier Women*, 43.
8. Huston Horn, *The Pioneers*. The Old West series (New York: Time-Life Books, 1974), 167.
9. Myres, *Westering Women*, 89.
10. Ibid., 90.
11. Dee Brown, *The Gentle Tamers: Women of the Old West* (Lincoln: University of Nebraska Press, 1958), 269.
12. Luchetti and Olwell, *Women of the West*, 48.
13. Viewed online at the Kansas State Historical Society's website.
14. Riley, *Female Frontier*, 188.
15. Gray, *Women of the West*, 79.
16. Myres, *Westering Women*, 233.
17. "Mary Lease," Spartacus Educational, http://www.spartacus.schoolnet.co.uk/USAleaseM.htm.
18. Gray, *Women of the West*, 143.
19. Ibid., 57.
20. Richard Stiller, *Queen of Populists: The Story of Mary Elizabeth Lease* (New York: Thomas Crowell, 1970), 66.

21. Ibid., 73.
22. Ibid., 96
23. Ibid., 109.
24. Ibid., 117.
25. A speech from 1890. "Wall Street Owns the Country," History Is a Weapon, http://www.historyisaweapon.com/defcon1/marylease.html.
26. Ibid., 126.
27. Ibid., 136.
28. Ibid., 147.
29. "Speech to the Women's Christian Temperance Union," History Is a Weapon, http://www.historyisaweapon.com/defcon1/marylease2.html.
30. Stiller, *Queen of Populists*, 169.
31. Ibid., 175.
32. Ibid., 134.
33. Ibid., 226.
34. Carry Nation, *The Use and Need of the Life of Carry A. Nation*, 1905, viewed at Project Gutenberg online, www.gutenberg.org/cache/epub/1485/pg1485.html.
35. Nation, *Use and Need*.
36. Fran Grace, *Carry A. Nation: Retelling the Life* (Bloomington: Indiana University Press, 2001), 48.
37. Nation, *Use and Need*.
38. Ibid.
39. Grace, *Carry A. Nation*, 138.
40. Ibid., 147.
41. Ibid., 180.
42. Ibid., 202–203.
43. Ibid., 165.
44. Nation, *Use and Need*.
45. Grace, *Carry A. Nation*, 221.
46. Ibid.
47. Ibid., 209.
48. Nation, *Use and Need*.
49. Grace, *Carry A. Nation*, 274.

Chapter 6: Clash of Cultures

1. Wilson, *'49er.*
2. Frances Roe, *Army Letters from an Officer's Wife* (1909; repr., Lincoln: University of Nebraska Press, 1981), 41.
3. Lydia Allen Rudd, 1852, quoted in Schlissel, *Women's Diaries*, 193, 195.
4. Knight, *Diary.*
5. Colt, *Went to Kansas.*
6. Susette La Flesche, quoted in Wilson, *Bright Eyes*, 335.
7. Rayna Green, *Women in American Indian Society: Indians of North America* (New York: Chelsea House Publishers, 1992), 69. (This quote has been attributed to several tribes, including the Cheyenne and the Blackfeet.)
8. Gray, *Women of the West*, 99.
9. Wilson, *Bright Eyes*, 151.
10. Roe, *Army Letters*, 96.
11. Carrington, *My Army Life*, 45.
12. Christina Phillips Campbell, 1858, quoted in Stratton, *Pioneer Women*, 116.
13. Myres, *Westering Women*, 77.
14. Wilson, *'49er.*
15. Rachel Plummer's book, *Rachel Plummer's Narrative of Twenty-One Months Servitude as a Prisoner Among the Comanche Indians,* quoted in S. C. Gwynne, *Empire of the Summer Moon: Quanah Parker and the Rise and Fall of the Comanches, the Most Powerful Indian Tribe in American History* (New York: Scribner, 2010), 17.
16. Ibid., 22.
17. Ibid.
18. Ibid., 38.
19. Ibid., 41.
20. Ibid., 42.
21. Ibid.
22. Plummer, quoted in Jo Ella Powell Exley, *Frontier Blood: The Saga of the Parker Family* (College Station: Texas A&M University Press, 2001), 75.

23. Plummer, quoted in Gwynne, *Empire*, 52.
24. Gwynne, *Empire*, 124.
25. Ibid., 84.
26. Quote from Banc's brother (ibid.,104).
27. Quote from Banc (ibid., 105).
28. Gwynne, *Empire*, 109.
29. Ibid., 116.
30. Ibid., 117.
31. Ibid., 184.
32. Ibid., 189.
33. Ibid., 192.
34. Quotes in this passage are taken from Sarah Winnemucca, *Life Among the Piutes: Their Wrongs and Claims,* http://www.yosemite.ca.us/library/life_among_the_piutes/malheur_agency.html. The book also appears in part in Luchetti and Olwell, *Women of the West*, 103–110.
35. Wilson, *Bright Eyes*, 335.
36. Ibid., 150.
37. Ibid., 180.
38. Ibid., 181–82.
39. Ibid., 217.
40. Ibid., 250.
41. Ibid.
42. Ibid., 326.

Chapter 7: Love Song to the West

1. Boyd, *Cavalry Life*, 176.
2. Ibid., 182.
3. Ibid., 183.
4. Ibid., 176.
5. Custer, *Tenting*, 2:381–82.
6. Stratton, *Pioneer Women*, 46.
7. Ibid., 56.
8. Willa Cather, *The Song of the Lark* (1915; repr., New York: Signet Classics, 1991), 191–92.

BIBLIOGRAPHY

Books

Armitage, Susan, and Elizabeth Jameson, eds. *The Women's West.* Norman: University of Oklahoma Press, 1987.

Bartley, Paula, and Cathy Loxton. *Plains Women: Women in the American West.* Cambridge: Cambridge University Press, 1991.

Benson, Maxine. *Martha Maxwell, Rocky Mountain Naturalist.* Lincoln: University of Nebraska Press, 1986.

Boyd, Frances. *Cavalry Life in Tent and Field.* 1894. Reprint, Lincoln: University of Nebraska Press, 1982.

Brown, Dee. *The Gentle Tamers: Women of the Old West.* Lincoln: University of Nebraska Press, 1958.

Bruyn, Kathleen. *"Aunt" Clara Brown: Story of a Black Pioneer.* Boulder: Pruett Publishing, 1970.

Butler, Anne M. *Daughters of Joy, Sisters of Misery: Prostitutes in the American West.* Chicago: University of Chicago Press, 1985.

Capps, Benjamin. *The Indians.* The Old West Series. New York: Time-Life Books, 1973.

Carrington, Frances. *My Army Life: A Soldier's Wife at Fort Phil Kearny.* 1910. Reprint, Boulder, CO: Pruett Publishing, 1990.

Craver, Rebecca McDowell. *The Impact of Intimacy: Mexican-Anglo Intermarriage in New Mexico, 1821–1846.* El Paso: Texas Western Press, 1982.

Custer, Elizabeth. *Boots and Saddles, or Life in Dakota with General Custer.* 1885. Reprint, Norman: University of Oklahoma Press, 1961.

———. *Following the Guidon.* Reprint, Norman: University of Oklahoma Press, 1966.

———. *Tenting on the Plains.* Reprint, Norman: University of Oklahoma Press, 1971.

Dempsey, David and Raymond Baldwin. *The Triumphs and Trials of Lotta Crabtree.* New York: William Morrow, 1968.

Exley, Jo Ella Powell. *Frontier Blood: The Saga of the Parker Family.* College Station: Texas A&M University Press, 2001.

Fischer, Christiane, ed. *Let Them Speak for Themselves: Women in the American West, 1849–1900.* Hamden, CT: Archon Books, 1977.

Grace, Fran. *Carry A. Nation: Retelling the Life.* Bloomington: Indiana University Press, 2001.

Gray, Dorothy. *Women of the West.* Millbrae, CA: Les Femmes Press, 1976.

Gwynne, S. C. *Empire of the Summer Moon: Quanah Parker and the Rise and Fall of the Commanches, the Most Powerful Indian Tribe in American History.* New York: Scribner, 2010.

Henry, Fern. *My Checkered Life: Luzena Stanley Wilson in Early California.* Nevada City, CA: Carl Mautz Publishing, 2003.

Horn, Huston. *The Pioneers.* The Old West Series. New York: Time-Life Books, 1974.

Jeffrey, Julie Roy. *Converting the West: A Biography of Narcissa Whitman.* Norman: University of Oklahoma Press, 1991.

———. *Frontier Women, The Trans-Mississippi West, 1840–1880.* New York: Hill and Wang, 1979.

Luchetti, Cathy, and Carol Olwell. *Women of the West.* New York: Orion Books, 1982.

Merington, Marguerite, ed. *The Custer Story: The Life and Intimate Letters of General George A. Custer and His Wife Elizabeth.* New York: Devin-Adair, 1950.

Myres, Sandra. *Westering Women and the Frontier Experience, 1800–1915.* Albuquerque: University of New Mexico Press, 1982.

Niethammer, Carolyn. *Daughters of the Earth: Lives and Legends of American Indian Women.* New York: Collier Books, 1977.

Rarick, Ethan. *Desperate Passage: The Donner Party's Perilous Journey West*. New York: Oxford University Press, 2008.

Riley, Glenda. *The Female Frontier: A Comparative View of Women on the Prairie and the Plains*. Lawrence: University Press of Kansas, 1988.

Roe, Frances. *Army Letters from an Officer's Wife*. 1909. Reprint, Lincoln: University of Nebraska Press, 1981.

Schlissel, Lillian. *Women's Diaries of the Westward Journey*. New York: Schocken Books, 1982.

Stiller, Richard. *Queen of Populists: The Story of Mary Elizabeth Lease*. New York: Thomas Y. Crowell, 1970.

Stratton, Joanna. *Pioneer Women: Voices from the Kansas Frontier*. New York: Simon and Schuster, 1981.

Summerhayes, Martha. *Vanished Arizona: Recollections of My Army Life*. 1908. Reprint, New York: J. B. Lippincott, 1963.

Wallace, Robert. *The Miners*. The Old West Series. New York: Time-Life Books, 1976.

Wilson, Dorothy Clarke. *Bright Eyes: The Story of Susette La Flesche, an Omaha Indian*. New York: McGraw-Hill Book, 1974.

Wyman, Walker. *Frontier Woman: The Life of a Woman Homesteader on the Dakota Frontier*. River Falls: University of Wisconsin Press, 1972.

Online Sources

Colt, Miriam Davis. *Went to Kansas*, 1862. http://www.kancoll.org/books/colt.

Knight, Amelia Stewart. *Diary of Mrs. Amelia Stewart Knight (1853)*. http://www.oregontrail101.com/00.ar.knight.html.

Lease, Mary Elizabeth. Speech. http://www.historyisaweapon.com/defcon1/marylease.html.

———. Speech. http://www.historyisaweapon.com/defcon1/marylease2.html.

Murphy, Virginia Reed. *Across the Plains in the Donner Party: A Personal Narrative of the Overland Trip to California*. http://onlinebooks.library.upenn.edu/webbin/book/lookupid?key=olbp24322.

Nation, Carry A. *The Use and Need of the Life of Carry A. Nation*, 1905. Project Gutenberg. http://www.gutenberg.org/cache/epub/1485/pg1485.html.

Wilson, Luzena Stanley. *'49er: Her Memoirs Taken Down by Her Daughter in 1881.* http://www.pbs.org/weta/thewest/resources/archives/three/luzena.htm.

Winnemucca, Sarah. *Life Among the Piutes: Their Wrongs and Claims, 1883.* http://www.yosemite.ca.us/library/life_among_the_Piutes/malheuragency.html.

INDEX

Page numbers in *italics* indicate pages with photographs.